Reading Life

Also by Sven Birkerts

My Sky Blue Trades:
Growing Up Counter in a Contrary Time

Readings

The Gutenberg Elegies: The Fate of Reading in an Electronic Age

American Energies: Essays on Fiction

The Electric Life: Essays on Modern Poetry

An Artificial Wilderness: Essays on Twentieth-Century Literature

EDITOR:

Tolstoy's Dictaphone: Technology and the Muse

The Evolving Canon

Writing Well, with Donald Hall

Reading Life

Books for the Ages

———•———

Sven Birkerts

Graywolf Press
SAINT PAUL, MINNESOTA

Publication of this volume is made possible in part by a grant provided by the Minnesota State Arts Board, through an appropriation by the Minnesota State Legislature; a grant from the Wells Fargo Foundation Minnesota; and a grant from the National Endowment for the Arts, which believes that a great nation deserves great art. Significant support has also been provided by the Bush Foundation; Target; the McKnight Foundation; and other generous contributions from foundations, corporations, and individuals. To these organizations and individuals we offer our heartfelt thanks.

Published by Graywolf Press
2402 University Avenue, Suite 203
Saint Paul, Minnesota 55114
All rights reserved.

www.graywolfpress.org

Published in the United States of America

ISBN 978-1-55597-464-0

2 4 6 8 9 7 5 3 1
First Graywolf Printing, 2007

Library of Congress Control Number: 2006929504

Cover art and design: Scott Sorenson

Acknowledgments

Grateful thanks to the editors of the publications listed below for first publishing the following essays:

"Love's Wound, Love's Salve: Knut Hamsun's *Pan*": *American Scholar* and *Re-Readings,* edited by Anne Fadiman (Farrar, Straus and Giroux, 2005).

"Romancing the Self: Gustave Flaubert's *Madame Bovary*": *American Scholar*

"'Live All You Can': Henry James's *The Ambassadors*": *The Threepenny Review*

"The Mad Energies of Art: Saul Bellow's *Humboldt's Gift*": *The Virginia Quarterly Review*

"The Possibility of the Search: Walker Percy's *The Moviegoer*": *The Believer*

For their patience, acumen, willingness to humor and say the necessary hard thing I want to thank Lynn Focht, Chris Benfey, Askold Melnyczuk, Liam Rector, Tom Sleigh, Tom Frick, Anne Fadiman, Wendy Lesser, Bill Pierce, Dinah Lenney, Ted Genoways, Heidi Julavits, Fiona McCrae, and Anne Czarniecki.

Contents

Reading Life

The Reading Life

WHEN I WAS YOUNGER, before books had sorted themselves into different kinds of experiences, I read a great deal. I read in all directions—for story, or because I was curious about a reputation, or hungered for some mood or atmosphere, or just because I had time on my hands and wanted to see where a particular path of words might take me. I miss those days, the excitement of wandering, that sense of the book as an unknown entity that could hold just about anything between its covers. For one of the sad consequences of reading many books for many years is that the map eventually starts to come clear, with fewer and fewer uncharted areas. And then with the passing of enough time the other thing disappears too, the languid leisure that is the spawning ground of the inner life. I don't ever now have time on my hands as I once did. The Protestant ethic has finally bent me to its will. Now when I do have any idleness it afflicts my conscience. What happened to simple being?

For any devoted reader the act is deeply, complexly bound up with inwardness—with consciousness, sensibility, with whatever noun we choose to designate the murmur of awareness that accompanies us—and carries us—from first waking to sleep again. The words we read—the impressions, the narratives, the conversations and thoughts of characters—not only touch our private sense of ourselves, but merge with it, shaping and directing it. After all, we use our own imaginative energy to bring the words to life and then project their content—their stuff—onto the interior screen. There the world we've generated from the written signals glows vividly, or flickers faintly, or moves in and out of resolution, depending on who we are, what we are reading, and the wattage of our moods.

WHAT IS IT THAT MAKES certain people become readers and others not? It's an ongoing mystery. Many people grow up in bookish environments and don't pick up the print addiction, while some of the fiercest book partisans had little or no early exposure whatsoever. It's hard to know what started them on their course. I opt for psychology over socialization: some people discover a deep gratification in the print transaction, others don't; certain temperaments are predisposed, most aren't. As for what determines the predisposition, I won't presume to generalize—it's hard enough for me to work down to the root of my own experience.

I believe that I came to reading out of a sense of solitary self-consciousness. This is the line connecting what I recall of my earliest childhood book-immersions with my life in the present. I don't mean that books were an answer to loneliness, not first and foremost, nor that they were a conventional ticket to imaginary other places (though I was hardly immune to the pleasures of transport). In fact, there are ways in which reading intensifies life in the here and now even as it takes us away. When I read, as I did obsessively, certain mysteries, like those in the Hardy Boys series, it was not just to lose myself inside the world of Frank and Joe Hardy. I was also taking the adrenaline of suspense and working it into my own life, borrowing from it, looking at my world through the frame of mystery. We've all done the filmmaker pantomime, forming a box with forefinger and thumb of both hands, peering at whatever is right in front of us as if we were getting ready to film. It's a simple vantage shift, a way of sharpening the sense of the thing by defamiliarizing it. I found early on that moving through my day under the compression of an author's imagination had a similar effect. It was a way of involving myself more deeply while working with a removed perspective, and it cut against the ache of solitariness.

MY BASIC FEELING of disconnectedness never disappeared, it just changed its aspect. When I was a teen I embraced the then-fashionable term "alienation." To be alienated was to be estranged, living askew. It was an intensified—and voluntarily accepted—version of what I had always felt. Living was dissonance; I registered a clear lack of harmony between inner and outer, between what I was thinking and feeling and what was required by the situation around me—by family, teachers and friends.

Solitary self-consciousness, the experience of distance, the stress of being angled to the world, as well as the cottony solace of alienation—all of these are part of the predisposition that leads to reading. But there is also a craving for whatever is not supplied by our worldly interactions, an intuition of other alignments, other scales of mattering, other possible tempos, almost as if turning pages and processing language produce a chemical surge in the system, some steadying vibration missing before.

I don't have specific memories about how I originally came into reading, except for one, very isolated, which was the jubilant, viscerally felt moment when a previously impenetrable line of print—the first sentence of Rudyard Kipling's *The Jungle Book*—opened to me like a hard knot suddenly yielding. I was in the first grade, but fifty years later I can still feel that sudden availability of meaning, and the realization that it was not just a phrase, a sentence, giving way before me, but a whole universe that until a moment before had been sealed off.

Otherwise, though, the transitions are murky, how I might have shifted from one level, one depth or capacity, to another. What's sure for me is that from that first cracking of the code I've never not been a reader; I've never moved too far away from that other reality made available by print. When I open a book, even now, I still have some expectation of changing my psychological vantage. But this is nothing like my earliest reading which, until I lost the power of that absorption, allowed what felt like an almost complete exchange of realities. What I feel these days is a strenuous give-and-take between perspectives, a tension between the immediacy of the present and the brightly conjured *there* of the book. What's more, it's generally not the erasure I crave, not complete vicariousness, but that peculiar doubleness, that oscillation between outer and inner. Something about energy—attention—moving between two poles, turning up the inner and dimming down the outer, compensates the imbalance, my sense of the world being, as William Wordsworth wrote, "too much with us."

Thrown too fully into the outer—the picnic, the parade, the dutiful social gathering—I panic. I find no place to put this self I tote around. When I settle in with a book, on the other hand, I feel the body and its behaviors recede. The cloudy "I" leaks out, expanding to fill whatever imagined space becomes available.

WHENEVER I GO BACK to memories of childhood reading I feel embarrassed in hindsight. The books I loved—and consumed—were not beyond literary reproach. I wasn't feasting early on excellence, and the part of me that regards reading with a judging eye, that thinks we can measure the quality of our inner life by what we do and don't respond to, wonders why not. I wasn't seeking out Charles Dickens and Robert Louis Stevenson. I found my way not to Thomas Hardy but to the Hardy Boys—those books that turned out, years later, not to have been written by Franklin W. Dixon, but by a team of hacks. Where was my discernment, my instinct for nuanced narrative and credibly complex characters? Well, it must not have existed because this one obsession kept me captive for a good long time. When I was in its deepest throes I would ask my mother to leave me off at the local Little Professor bookstore when she went to do her shopping. I would stand, often for an hour or more, in front of the Hardy Boys section, that crazy-making yard or so of blue spines, holding whichever book I was reading close to my face, paging my way forward as quickly as I could—the classic nerd.

This was certainly reading—it was part of my long apprenticeship to the act—but what was the point of it? Escape and intensification, as I've suggested. I pulled this world of the Hardys around me 360 degrees, and I breathed its air. I worked up every scene in detail until I *saw* it, felt it, set it pulsing with my own speeded-up heartbeat, following the adventures until they streamed one into the next, my reading become a grand banquet of clues, dangers, and last-minute rescues. That this could be endlessly varied without the brothers or their friends ever getting older or losing their joking camaraderie, and without their father, the esteemed Fenton Hardy, ever faltering in his wise surveillance of their endeavors, was unbelievable delight.

Easy as it is to recover the first enchantment, I don't remember how I finally outgrew the whole business. There was fading, gradual distance, a lessening of investment, and finally one day there was something new to attract the attention. Oddly, once I'd left the Hardy brothers behind, I seldom gave them a thought. Decades sluiced by, and it was really only when my own son Liam got to mid-grade school that I zeroed in again. Suddenly I felt that I wanted to give it to him, the gift of those books, what I remembered as being a thrilling and sustainable imaginary world. By this point, Liam and I were in our last period of bedtime reading, there more for the sentimental ritual than anything else. He had already begun to enjoy reading for himself. But we still put in our time with Harry Potter. In fact, it was just when we had finally finished one of the Potters and were looking around for the next thing that I thought to introduce the Hardys.

What a dull thud that was. Not just for Liam, who humored me for a week or so before announcing that he wasn't that interested, but for me, too. If reading aloud had an equivalent to chewing a cud, this was it. I couldn't believe the formulaic barrenness, the machine-made dialogue, the pat predictability of the characters and plot turns. This couldn't be right. "Wait," I said, "wait until Chet Morton comes in—he's a funny character." Well, Chet arrived, but he was as bad as the brothers. I could feel Liam's brave attention drifting. And then I closed the covers. As Dante wrote, apropos of Paolo and Francesca: "We read no more that day."

READING IN OUR YOUNGER YEARS is an evolutionary process, I think, closely tied to the expansion and deepening of awareness, practical knowledge, and social sophistication, and as experience sharpens us, allowing us to bring more and more to the encounter, so it helps influence how we absorb the events that come our way. During adolescence my reading had a good deal to do with the kinds of situations I encountered. If I hadn't read, say, *On the Road* or *The Tropic of Cancer* when I did, I might have made a number of different choices. And even if I *had* thrown myself into hitchhiking in every direction, or wandering Europe with a backpack, I would have brought to bear a different pressure of romantic imagining, and every situation would have unfolded otherwise.

The movements from phase to phase—in reading as in life—are often gradual, marked by little shifts in our attention patterns. When the juice, the savor, began to leak away from the old reliable Hardy scenario, it was replaced by what felt like an irresistible new excitement. This was the early 1960s. We had a handsome young president who was also witty and articulate, and who told an interviewer from the press that he enjoyed reading Ian Fleming's James Bond novels. Suddenly those books were everywhere, at newsstands, in revolving drugstore racks, and even though they were deemed too racy for young teens, everyone I knew was reading them. Access was not a problem. There they sat on the home coffee table. *The Spy Who Loved Me, Dr. No, Goldfinger, On Her Majesty's Secret Service* . . . It's hard now to give Bond back his pre-Connery aura, hard, indeed, to repossess the time-bound glamour of those crisp little paperbacks with their sketchily suggestive covers, which we only glanced at. Our interest was taken up mainly by the sexy bits (with Bond always getting right to the brink of something really good), the exhilarating sophistication of the trappings (the drinks, cars, clothes, gizmos), and the steady dose of international intrigue (signaled by exotic cities, secret bank-accounts) that had as much influence as the Huntley-Brinkley news hour on giving us the sense of the dangerous larger world.

But Ian Fleming was important to my reading story in another, more lasting way. Although he was not in any sense a legitimate author of the sort I would soon be studying in English classes—not even a John Steinbeck or a William Golding—it was while I was reading the Bond books that the spark first leapt the gap between the idea of *writer* and the idea of *book*. Of course I'd made the connection before—books came from writers as milk came from cows—but this time it happened in a fatefully romantic way. I finally "got" that being an author of books was not only an actual vocation, but a highly attractive one. For this I credit my mother.

My mother read—by day, by night, whenever time allowed, and with palpable devotion. It was her books that filled the upstairs bookcases and gave me a quiet sense of bounty whenever I lingered there to inspect, reading dust-jacket descriptions, poring over author photos.

Ian Fleming was one of my mother's writer-heroes. Not because of his literary skills, which she conceded as nothing remarkable, but because, like Hemingway, he conformed to a basic type: he was handsome in the rugged, manly way she liked, romantically erratic, cosmopolitan, and literarily productive. He married adventure—the outward life—to output; he was dashing. Best of all: he was the favorite of another of her idealized males, John F. Kennedy. I remember that she kept a copy of Fleming's travelogue *Thrilling Cities* on her night table for the longest time, and the book became a talisman for me. When no one was home, I would sit on the edge of my parents' bed and page through the descriptions of Singapore, Cairo, Rio . . .

Reading Fleming in tandem with my friends—those few who read— I was mainly focused on intrigue and sexual innuendo. But I was also slowly coming around to the conception that being a writer was in itself a heroic thing, laying the groundwork for a mythology that remains with me to this day. Writer as creator, writer as witness, writer as person living an engaged authentic life—not that I have ever measured up to my own high standard of authenticity.

It was another stage. As I'd done with the Hardy Boys, I went through my days screening everything through the mesh of my grandiose Fleming imaginings, giving situations and encounters the italics of fresh emphasis. The difference was that now I had also begun to see this angling of experience as an attribute of my eventual vocation—for in all of this it had become clear to me, though I don't remember exactly how, that I was destined to be a writer.

From the time of my early teen years, I spent as much time as I could in bookstores and libraries, not only because books offered stimulus to my writerly fantasies, but also because they reached me in some more abstract way. When I was near shelves of books, I came alive, almost as if I were picking up emanations. I felt a sense of perspective, of scale, the solace of the idea of generations, as well as a great desire to do things on my own, to achieve.

If tales of mystery and intrigue originally lured me into the other world of reading, and if Ian Fleming gave me my first intoxicating glimpse of author as protagonist, hero of the double life, then the melancholy brooding of later adolescence redirected me completely. In my early teens I had my first exposure to J. D. Salinger, to the character of Holden Caulfield. This was something I hadn't imagined possible, that I could open the pages of a dimestore paperback and merge, from the first sentence on, with a voice that seemed to be coming not from outside, but from my own restless core. Here was absorption—identification—of a very different kind. Now instead of projecting myself into the doings of an idealized protagonist, I was taken over, involved with a character not through action, through his deeds, but through his basic way of being, his attitude. Everything changed. Where before I would pilfer for myself the whole dramatic frame, the concept, using it to magnify and intensify my own daily doings—seeing situations as potentially fraught with danger, mystery, or unexpected romantic development—now I felt my overall attitude and outlook profoundly affected by that of the character I was reading. I was, in a light and mostly benign sense of the word, possessed. Holden Caulfield was the first—his phrases, his slangy cadences, his poignant bemused wondering at things were like a viral infection: overnight large parts of my life became "depressing as hell" and half the people I dealt with were suddenly unmasked to me as "phonies." Although I was hardly alone in this—a whole generation was undergoing a Salinger baptism—I imagined myself alone. I had to. Holden himself would have had nothing but scorn for the idea of a Holden craze.

After such exposure, such moving around of the inner furniture, I couldn't go back to the *status quo ante* again. The voice, the feeling of connection—even if it was a connection to disaffection—had created an appetite. I began to cast around in my reading for other books that could give me that same moody pleasure. Action and adventure didn't interest me anymore. James Bond couldn't hope to compete with this skinny chain-smoking teenager with his red deerstalker hat.

Holden initiated the grail quest for the credible literary antihero. This figure, this filter of experience, had to accept my projections. He—a female character would not do—had to be thoughtful, sad, isolated from the herd of others around him; he had to know his existence as problematic, painful even, much as I did (surrounded as I was by phonies). So I read, and enjoyed, books like *P.S. Wilkinson* by C. D. B. Bryan, *The Sterile Cuckoo* by John Nichols, *The Temple of Gold* by William Goldman, *A Separate Peace* by John Knowles, and others, the names and jacket images of which have begun to fade from memory.

I was, at fifteen and sixteen, I see this now, nibbling at the fringes of a more serious literary involvement, one that would lead me soon enough to the Eugene Gant novels of Thomas Wolfe, to Henry Miller, Jack Kerouac, Knut Hamsun, J. P. Donleavy, and then Ernest Hemingway, F. Scott Fitzgerald, Joyce Cary—anything, really, that had a whiff of the angst or rebellion I needed in order to keep working on my complicated self-definition.

AT SOME POINT the reading experience changes—the discovery curve flattens and it gets harder and harder to tap the old reliable pleasures. The reader gets jaded. At least this was my experience. By the time I entered my forties I'd been reading steadily for more than twenty-five years—on my own, as a student, as a teacher, as a reviewer. I had worked full-time in bookstores for nearly a decade, giving and getting recommendations, dipping my nose into thousands of books. My approach to reading novels changed accordingly. If I had less expectation about discovering the pure unknown, I also became far more receptive to the idea of re-reading. There were some good reasons for this. For one thing, I was less subject than before to the tyranny of the checklist—being able to say, to myself, to others, that I had read such and such a book. That powerful old incentive had begun to fade a bit. For another, I was now in most cases far enough from my original reading to have forgotten many things about that encounter. Indeed, I was often surprised, going back, to find the work had grown fresh again, full of unexpected turns and nuances.

Although I returned to many novels during this time, there is a small group that, for whatever complex reasons, acquired special status. These were works I thought of covetously, as private properties. I felt that I had a special connection to them. Not only had I filled them with my most intense projections, but I also knew that they had more to tell me.

I ended up re-reading some of these special books a number of times, in part to recapture something of the pleasure they had given me, but also, I now realize, because I found that they served me as reference points. They were like so many buoys of the inner life, allowing me to mark changes and get a sense of distances traversed.

This involved a double measurement. The novels themselves, of course, reflected different psychological interests—the trajectory from *The Catcher in the Rye* to *The Ambassadors* is a long one—but my reactions over time to the same work also inscribed a pattern of growth and change. Reengaging these key books in my forties, I was a better, more astute reader, no question. But I was also *different.* On every level. I no longer responded to language, or character, or ideas as I had at twenty, or thirty. My sense of what was funny, or poignant was different, too. As was the frame, the context within which I now faced the work. When I read *Madame Bovary* for the first time, I was nineteen years old and staying in a bunkhouse in Montana. I had little understanding of European history, or French mores, or the traditions of the novel; I had no conception of the literal meaning or the aesthetic implications of the Flaubertian *mot juste.* I knew a bit about sexual passion but nothing at all of marriage, and so on.

Before taking up the question of re-reading, I should say more about the incentives and circumstances of many of those first exposures. I mean here my reading of the familiar "classics" and the checklist mentality that was so hard to shake off. I was, I should confirm, an early and unquestioning believer in the edifying power of books that had withstood the "test of time," and question this as I have over the years, I have never lost the basic faith. Others had religion in the home, I had this: books enlarge and improve; they humanize. I accept this even as I am without proof, for I have never found a shred of bankable concrete evidence—not in my own character anyway. And what would such evidence amount to? It's a peculiar business. If I undertake a regimen of exercise I see the good of it in a matter of days. But if someone challenges me to prove that a lifetime of reading has bettered me, I'm lost. Bettered how? I have a larger vocabulary than I might have otherwise, sure. And I can talk for hours about fictional situations and characters, using various refined terminologies. But has any of this has made me "better" than I might have been otherwise? In fact, I could easily imagine the opposite argument: all this immersion has undermined my practical readiness, I have distanced myself from my own primary emotions, all my work has fitted me for a career of reading and writing about books and not much else.

I try not to take this latter accusation too seriously. I don't really accept the idea that the point of living is to contend with practical matters, or that direct emotion always has primacy over more refracted and complicated kinds of response. In my view a command of various perspectives and psychological vantages is an enormous asset in the social world. How can it not be? But I should also admit that I keep a residual trace of doubt, the original source of which is, no question, my father thundering at me that I should leave off my ineffectual—escapist—turning of pages and mow the lawn.

Slight hesitations notwithstanding, the idea of the importance of the classics lodged in my susceptible superego early on, and there it remains. At first I took it on the authority of my elders—teachers and credible public spokesmen—as well as canonizing institutions like the Modern Library. Isn't this how many of us get our ideas of the "classic" and the canonical, absorbing them through sustained cultural cross-referencing? An English teacher, himself a product of this process, refers in class to the "great" Southern novelist William Faulkner, winner of the Nobel Prize for Literature (obviously prizes matter), whereupon soon after we meet with the same name cited as an influence in a headnote for some other writer we are to read. By the time Faulkner's novels turn up in a roster of "other Modern Library classics" or some such, the deed is done. We accept the greatness on faith, without having read the man; we are—possibly—ready to blame ourselves and not our sources if we find the work uninteresting or incomprehensible.

Maybe because of my mother, or because of the general family climate—veneration of the greatness of artists and thinkers was a given—I became fixated on lists of "great books" early on. I conceived them as so many ladders I had to climb and imagined that successful ascent would remake me. Into what? Some blue-blazered Alistair Cooke figure, a hot-triggered pundit like William Buckley? I don't think I had many models in my early years of apprenticeship, except for a few of the brainy seniors I admired when I enrolled as a new fifth-former at the prep school down the road. But who can judge the true power of such influence? A knowing classroom reference to Herodotus by a blazer-wearing prefect (we had prefects, blazers!) could be ignition enough under the right circumstances. And a few of these exemplars did exist. As did various underemployed "masters" (teachers) who had their sights set on bigger things than teaching, and took out their intellectual frustrations on us, bullying us and mocking our inadequacy.

Whatever the causes, and however it all worked, from my teenage years on I was haunted by the enormity of what I didn't know, and I had a strong determination to make inroads. It was a short-lived, but intense, pleasure to strike a line through another title on one of those lists. *Of Human Bondage* by W. Somerset Maugham—check. *Sons and Lovers*—check. Nor has the compulsion died out completely. I'd be lying if I pretended I felt no private back-slap of accomplishment when, fairly recently, I made it all the way to the end of Henry James's *The Ambassadors*. And I admit that I do from time to time still linger over some census of importance, muttering in my thoughts, Achebe, Chinua, *Things Fall Apart*—check.

For all this, I always refused to read slavishly, or follow any approved sequence. It mattered to me that I be engaged by a book, interested, that I'd wanted to read it. My whole literary education has been a process of trying to become the person who would *want* to read Classic X. If I felt no pull toward the work of Haldor Laxness, say, then it was because I wasn't yet cultured enough to be curious about rural Icelandic life. Samuel Butler, Sir Thomas Browne? My historical horizons were still too narrow, my reach of reference impoverished. To study a list was to shuttle incessantly between self-congratulation and self-reproach—it was a way of rating myself against the measuring wall of my own ideals.

SOMEHOW THROUGH ALL of this, because of it, in spite of it, all kinds of books got read, approved "classics" among them, and when enough years had passed I did begin to get that sense of the field narrowing. I was going for longer and longer intervals without connecting to a novel that stirred me up or repositioned the world for me. At the same time, for reasons I've given, books that had once worked their spell on me started to look appealing again.

With return came the first great surprise of re-reading, the recognition that there is no stepping twice into the same print river. This is something more profound than the traveler remarking that the houses seem smaller, the trees differently placed, though on occasion this is what it feels like, too. More often, though, and especially with the more ambitious books, came the head-shaking recognition that everything was changed, that I could not have been present in this world before, at least not fully aware. And with this I would sometimes get a metaphysical intuition: I had moved somehow closer to understanding the mystery of literature. Literature is not, as represented by institutions, as regarded by criticism—indeed, as symbolized by the solid bound object—a fixed unchanging entity. The work is no more a static thing than the reader is a reliably constant presence. If anything, the reverse is true. While the words may be locked into place, held fast, their valences are untethered, and it is only the reader's responsiveness, playing over them like a wind, that determines in what ways and to what degree a work will *mean*. What a thought! It is so against our systems, our habits and assumptions, that we find it hard to grasp. Reading, the mind's traffic in signs and signifiers, is the most dynamic, changeful, and possibly transformational act we can imagine. To have read a work and have been strongly affected by it—and to then come back to it after many years—can be a foundation-shaking event.

But this truth is not easy to catch hold of, much less assess and evaluate. There is no way to escape the workings of indeterminacy. The experimenter is, as Heisenberg long ago observed, part of the experiment, a factor in its result. So with re-reading—we have no neutral place from which to consider our findings. We may have responded one way when we read a novel twenty years ago, but unless we wrote down the particulars of that response, we have only our memories to go by—memories both elastic and unreliable. I may remember that I loved the mood of the opening passage of a Thomas Hardy novel, I may even remember, or think I remember, specific details. On return I discover that the section is really only a few paragraphs long, and that the best details have been edited out—not a trace of that winding path I pictured so vividly. You can see where the problem lies—not with the difference between first and second responses, but with memory itself, with the fact that much of that first response has vanished into an imprecise, partly invented, retelling. What my re-reading brings me up against is not necessarily a changed perception of the work, but a recognition of the falsifying—the transformational—power of memory.

If my memory is not especially instructive about my first experience of *The Return of the Native,* it does tell me a great deal about my imagination and my projections. Nor are we dealing with some single instance. The complete re-reading of that, or any other, novel lays down layer after layer of these corrections, or self-revisions, and in their accumulation they become a fuzzy, often inscrutable interior self-portrait. Most often, I look up from this strange exposure augmented. I feel that I have grown, become more discerning, smarter, capable of finer psychological insight. If I respond with what I imagine is equal enthusiasm, I feel vindicated. If my response is diminished, less enthusiastic, I chalk it up to maturity, though I may—as happened with Jack Kerouac's *On the Road* after several decades—also wonder if I have not traded away a certain susceptibility.

RE-READING—THE GOING BACK, the reiteration—is what gets us deeper into what reading is because it forces us to let go of the idea of text as static, or stable, in its meanings, and of ourselves as simple translators of written signs into contents. Re-reading immerses us in the dynamic of change and indeterminacy, and in the process more closely merges our reading and the inner life, for in going back to a book we can't help reconnecting with our prior subjectivities. Focused though we may be, we are not seeing just the text in front of our eyes. No matter how thoroughly the passing of time may have erased the traces of the earlier encounter, some expectations remain. And these become, inevitably, the screen through which we take in the narration. We re-read the way we walk a once-known path, playing off what we see in front of us against what we expect: a turn, a hill, a brambly patch.

BUT ALL THIS REFLECTION on re-reading also forces a closer, more exacting look at the novel itself, at the particular pleasure and discipline of novel-reading, which is different from other kinds of reading, certainly the informational kind—histories, biographies, and topical books. What is the "genius" or spirit of the form that makes it so unlike all other creative expressions? I've been pushed to wonder about this lately. There is a new piece of received wisdom in our culture: the factual, the nonfictional, has carried the day; events in the real world are more compelling and attention-worthy than anything we can invent. Some of our leading journals, former literary strongholds like the *Atlantic Monthly, Esquire,* and the *Paris Review,* have moved to scale back fiction in order to make room for more documentary reportage. Here it is the short story taking the hit, but the literary novel is faring just as badly in the precincts of publishing. Indeed, to call something "literary" in these circles is to call it unsalable. Marketing, however, is not the problem. What is finally at issue is nothing less than the status, the perceived value, of imagination itself.

There is a widespread misapprehension about the nature and purpose of fiction, the novel in particular. A great many people still take storytelling to be the core mission of the novel, storytelling and the depiction of the features of our common world. If this were actually true, who would contest that the genre has been superceded? As Philip Roth observed decades ago, in our era of the extraordinary unthinkable real, the narration of what actually takes place, done with documentary precision, readily trumps what the novelist might cook up. What's more, nonfiction has the cachet of having actually happened. Likewise, the psychological possibilities available to the biographer, memoirist, and even the historian, are every bit as compelling as what the novelist conjures—and again, they are real. Obviously, so long as point-for-point comparisons of this kind are made, the score falls lopsidedly to the team of the actual.

But setting the invented and the "real" side by side in this way completely misses the point. It takes verisimilitude as a criterion of value and assumes that the reading of fiction and documentary nonfiction call on the same mental and psychological processes. Nothing could be less true.

The novel does not represent the world so much as it *creates* one that may or may not recall the one we know. Its value lies not in its fidelity to the known, but in its power to compel belief in a reality that differs from the known, the reality of "as if." The arena of fiction is, and always has been, the conjectural. Reading, we release our suppressed dreaming selves in ways that we cannot when we are constrained by the claim of the actual. The prototype of fiction, of "make believe," is the "Once upon a time" of the early romance, of the bedtime story. The documentary work would likely specify, "On the third of April, in 1986 . . ." The former opens us to wondering; the latter offers certainty, the reassurance of groundedness. Although I deliberately choose these polarized expressions, the simple truth is that fiction and nonfiction call upon, and appeal to, separate parts of the reader's sensibility.

It doesn't matter that the world outdoes the storyteller's imagination in terms of the characters and situations it throws up. What matters is that we read even the wildest nonfictional account in a different way than we read a work of fiction. Although the points of divergence may be hard to specify, they are vital. Consider the analogy to photography and representational painting. The photograph of a tree, say, and a carefully executed painting of the same. How are they distinguished—on the wall, and in our looking? The photo carries the authority of the actual: *this* is how the tree really looks. The painting, superficially anyway, is evaluated according to how close it comes to the same "actual." But only superficially. Where the photo is understood to be a composed transfer of the real, an artistically executed visual excerpt, the painting, however accurate in its delineation, is not a transfer but a translation. The subject matter has passed through the medium of the painter's interior awareness—it has been seen, absorbed, and reconstituted. There is a difference for the viewer. However beautiful the photo, however much its subject matter encourages private associations—our readily induced reveries of the pastoral—those projections run alongside, parallel to, the image. They do as much as would any dreamy thoughts we had looking at a real tree in a real field. With the painting, however, our subjective responses are directly circuited through the work. We are not responding to the seen "fact" of the tree, but to the rendering of the tree, which is already flush with the artist's own subjectivity. We are, in looking and reacting, in a communion of sorts with the vision—the interiority—of the artist.

The subjectivity of the photographer is present as well, but we look past it, much as we look past the artistic sensibility of the nonfiction writer, immersing ourselves instead in the *what* of the subject matter.

This, for me, is also the deep-rooted appeal of the novel, the world created with reference to the real, but at the same time apart from it. Reading an imagined work, I am released from contingent into conditional space. I move into the totality of the writer's inwardness as into a unique gravitational field. Every element of the book matters, not just the plot and the characters and the thematic development, but also the descriptions, digressions, sentence rhythms, everything. All the literary elements combine to create the distinctive "other" reality of the novel, and reading is not just following the narrative, but submitting to the full reach of that reality.

This self-contained density helps explain to me why I can't just take up one new novel after the next, even when the reading urge is on me. It also may account for why so many people like to stay with the familiar, reading in the vicinity of a favorite author. Because entering a new force field is taxing, requires a certain giving over of the self, not only in the sense of suspending disbelief on behalf of the narrative premise, but in terms of acclimatizing the self to a new atmosphere. The transfer has to "take." We all know the difference between reading with and against the grain, following the sympathies versus exerting the will.

To understand the novel in this way is also to begin to appreciate how specific books can affect us as they do, reaching us in the moment, but also exerting subtle ongoing effect. For when we submit to an author's terms, her vision, we take it in as experience. Because we absorb the actual detailed features of another's subjectivity, the work touches us at our most receptive, least barricaded, and we respond much as we do when we are affected by another individual. Except with this difference: the literary encounter, because it is conditional, not contingent, not binding, allows us an unconstrained response. Able to explore our feelings without committing to anything, we take the true measure of our own deeper disposition.

Characters can thus touch us profoundly. I don't think I exaggerate if I affirm that I have been as much affected by D. H. Lawrence's Rupert Birkin, or Virginia Woolf's Mrs. Ramsay, or Saul Bellow's Charlie Citrine, as I have by any number of flesh-and-blood people in my life. How does this influence work and what are the deeper dynamics of interaction? Real people affect me by way of their presence and by my response to their actions and views. The degree to which they remain with me is determined by the degree to which these energies press upon or modify my own deep-seated ways of being. I have spent hundreds of hours with people who have not left a mark on me at all. By the same token, through whatever operations of identification or projection, I feel that Mrs. Ramsay in *To the Lighthouse* has been one of the profound presences in my life. Woolf has made me privy to her perceptions and emotions, to the rhythms of her thought-process; through her represented consciousness I have known the grain of her most private awareness. I can bring her—or "her"—in close almost effortlessly. I wonder who I have ever known in this way and what I have known. What does it mean for my knowledge that Mrs. Ramsay is a created character? Is it necessarily inferior to the speculative half-knowing I have had with some of my work colleagues?

What is at issue here, obviously, is the reality status of fiction, and this is a philosophical inquiry having everything to do with the nature of knowing itself, with epistemology. The fact that I can't definitively answer my own questions makes the issue no less central. The questions are vexing because they are, at the deepest level, about the transactions between the self and others. They are psychological and phenomenological. They confirm, if anything, the profound complexity of serious literary engagement, and no argument about the primacy of documentary reportage—how the facts of the world are more fantastic than anything the writer can invent—lessens their impact.

THIS BRINGS ME AROUND to my concealed point of departure, the instigating quote that first sparked off these thoughts, which I had thought to use as my epigraph and then set aside. But it wouldn't stay suppressed; it surfaced again, insisting.

I found the quote, three sentences from philosopher Gabriel Marcel, in the opening section of Denis Donoghue's *The Arts Without Mystery:* "A problem . . . is something met with which bars my passage. It is before me in its entirety. A mystery, on the other hand, is something in which I find myself caught up, and whose essence is therefore not to be before me in its entirety. . . ."

Neither Marcel nor Donoghue were writing about reading specifically, but when I found the sentences they felt like a sudden illumination. I was struck first by the distinction made between the problem and the mystery, with the clear sense that mystery partakes of the essential, represents a philosophical category of sorts, and, second, by the idea of being caught up in something that is incomplete, obscure in its totality, still to be determined. How apt that seemed to serious reading, the act as I wanted to consider it, as open, intransitive, undertaken with the deep self invested and at stake.

Reading *is* open, in the world, in life, because reading is the most complex and volatile way we've found to merge the experienced and the imagined. Turning the pages of a challenging novel we spark up not just our intellect, but also our emotional and our dreaming selves. For no matter how precise the author's language, or how explicit the directives, we address the work according to what we need. It is very much an image of our own imagination we encounter, though it is constrained at every point by the narrowed possibilities offered by the text.

I wonder now why it took me so long to come to this, why I denied the deeper importance of re-reading even as I threw myself at it so zealously. Possibly I believed, as most survivors of higher education believe, that a book is somehow used up, finished, by our reading; that it is a device, spring-loaded with themes and characters, which discharges itself fully as we finish, and that anything else—our memories and references—constitutes a kind of dreamlike residue. I no longer think so. Reading infiltrates. Books stay alive, not just in the active imagination, but in the very structures of our awareness. Indeed, I begin to believe that plot, character, and theme, those staple values of the English courses, are the least of the business. They are—if I exaggerate it's only slightly—more a vehicle than the final point of the act. They are the precondition, the necessary pretext, for our absorption of the author's sensibility—the structure of her language, the atmospheric pressure of her subjectivity, the texture of her vision of the world. The reader takes this vision in through every description, every syntactical decision, every orchestrated transition. And while the action stops and the characters are dismissed to their undisclosed future lives, the feeling of that intense presiding presence remains. It cannot be concluded, even if the situations themselves are. Its mysterious chemical life continues.

Here, I think, re-reading discloses its ulterior nature—it is not only the reestablishing of a connection with a set of scenarios once vivid in the mind, a way of checking back in with the imagining self, but is also a way of refreshing a voice, a tonality, that has very likely faded. Faded, but not vanished completely. The decision to re-read a book is not usually an amnesiac's search for clues about what is lost. More likely it is prompted by some flaring up of memory, by a longing to be immersed again in a feeling that we know was important, gratifying, or somehow defining. We return, often, out of curiosity, no question, but also in the hope that something will be given back to us, or reawakened.

Lolita is one novel I go back to every few years. I know it well, if not line by line, then certainly scene by scene. The twists of plot are inscribed in memory, as are the continually changing dynamics of the characters, dynamics that cover a spectrum from lustful anticipation to the most rending sorrow. I don't need to go back to the book in order to remind myself of any part of the story. I am after something else, something my inner man needs as much as the body needs its potassium or zinc. I require the very particular flavor of the Nabokovian atmosphere, that unique blend of attuned poetic perception, world weariness, mordant dark humor, and desire. This was the note, the vibration, the sustained tonality that so delighted me—so answered me—when I first encountered it and that lodged in me until it became something I wanted to emulate. But though the feeling of it never left me, it did eventually begin to grow dim. I found I needed another dose, another plunge. I was confirmed. When I put myself back in its force field, I had the sharp sensation of stepping back into myself, of return.

This is not to say that Humbert Humbert is some proxy or other self, or that my worldview is his. Thankfully it's not. But the self is thickly, confusingly layered. Under the rubric of a single salient identity, we are many, one transparency grafted upon another. Reading Nabokov's novel brings certain parts of my nature forward: it makes me feel dark and ardent and full of sad human wisdom. Other novels tap other selves. As Ralph Waldo Emerson wrote: "Our moods do not know one another." No less essential parts of the self thrill with comparable delight to the fatalism of *Madame Bovary,* or the more fluid lyric surges of Woolf, or the muzzy psychological shifts of *The Ambassadors.*

Sometimes I think that the long-term work of reading is to discover, one by one, the books that hold the scattered elements of our nature, after which the true consummation can begin. We undertake the gradual focused exploration, nuance by nuance, of their meanings, their implications; we follow out the strands that mysteriously connect the words of another with the unformulated stuff of the self.

Children's Crusade

J.D. Salinger's *The Catcher in the Rye*

A LL OF US WHO LOVE *The Catcher in the Rye* love it in our own special way—or imagine we do—for the nature of the bond with this book is that it feels like a private place, a sanctum custom-fitted to the contours of every unique alienation and holding for each of us our noblest and most wounded sense of ourselves. Since its first publication in 1951—the year of my birth—narrator Holden Caulfield has been *the* template figure for the American adolescent, far more than James Dean or Elvis Presley or any later morosely sneering teen icon, and his voice remains the truest record of what it feels like to be young and misunderstood. The boy has extraordinary staying power. Much of the counterculture sensibility of the 1960s could be said to have emerged from under his red hunting cap. And the spell continues. My fifteen-year-old daughter now claims it as her favorite novel, and when she recently cited Holden as her most admired character in a school-application essay, the admissions director smiled, observing, "He certainly is a popular choice."

So much intense adoration, and so many different ways to try to reach the secret. Except that I don't know that it can be reached. For all the vast cultural influence of the novel, I can't think of a single piece of criticism that captures the nuances, and I hold out no high hopes for my own success. Indeed, it may just be that *Catcher's* elusiveness, its resistance to literary vivisection, is what helps assure that it will be fresh from generation to generation. I think of the old law: to pin a thing down is to begin the

process of its disenchantment. The last thing I want to do, then, is to turn
J. D. Salinger's novel into an object of study. I don't want to take it apart,
or compare it to anything, or harness the power of its disaffection for my
own purposes. I just want to set myself up near it and to think about the
pleasure it has given, and to use it to contemplate this business of youth
and alienation.

I was about fourteen when I read *Catcher* for the first time, and I'm
convinced that for me to grasp the book I have to reconnect with who
I was at the time of first contact. This is no small task. Every such approach to the past is a kind of stalking, requiring all sorts of psychological cunning and care. As I discovered several years ago when I set out
to write a coming-of-age memoir, our truest memories are often embedded in the most unlikely places, with our stray uncorrupted sensations—
uncorrupted because overlooked—holding the real key to what we felt
and how we viewed the world. These sensations, I've learned, less from
reading Vladimir Nabokov and Marcel Proust than from my own experience, are rarely encountered directly; they are mainly happened upon
through following subtle chains of association.

Writing that memoir, I also grasped that not every part of my younger
life would yield itself to recollection with equal ease. I found that I could
reliably tap certain seasons of boyhood and, say, the years of later adolescence, but there were other times, the in-drawn years of transformation—
junior high school—that were locked away like the prophecies of the
ancients. What was the world like when I was thirteen and fourteen years
old? Who was the person—the boy—who lay cornered in bed, as far away
from the world as he could get, boring into Salinger's novel as if it held
the deepest secrets of the life to come?

I remember I first got wind of the book from Kim Swift. Kim was
my great friend in those years, my first point of contact with some of the
more enticing mysteries of growing up. He had an older brother, Bill,
who was in the navy, and who once or twice a year came home wearing a
port-city aura of liquor, gambling, and after-hours fun. Bill was somehow
the herald of all that lay in store for us. And indeed, it was his copy of
Catcher that I first saw in Kim's room, the old Signet paperback (I have

an identical copy on my desk now) with a cover illustration of a young man with a suitcase standing in front of a neon-lit strip club, while a red-lipsticked woman of clearly questionable virtue lights a cigarette in the background.

Staring at that cover now, reading the boxed blurb—"This unusual book may shock you, will make you laugh, and may break your heart—but you will never forget it"—I can almost catch the feel of the original occasion, the afternoon almost forty years ago when I noticed the book lying on Kim's bed and, nearsighted even then, brought it up close for inspection. The image still holds the faint glow of that moment, and when I look at it now I can understand why some collectors collect. They are, at least the sentimental ones, hoping to re-experience the *frisson* of first connection, putting live sensation in front of thought and feeling the short-lived click of the world falling back into its old place.

I can't make the leap to any such perfect moment with *Catcher* right now, but I find something in the cover artist's attempt at luridness that brings me in closer than of my other attempts at recovery. Before I borrowed Kim's copy and started reading, I had a sharply brushed-in fantasy of a young man heading for the very first time into the exciting urban nightside of things, and the association has never completely vanished.

WHEN I READ THAT COPY of *Catcher* I was in the eighth grade at Berkshire Junior High School, and the world could not have looked different than it looks now. The hallways were rigged out with fun-house mirrors that skewed and twisted everything; fears and fantasies alike were blown up large and set to floating. My parents would lean in nightly to inspect the stranger who now had my place at the table. For it had arrived, right on schedule—though I didn't know there *was* a schedule—my undeniable otherness, the overpowering feeling that is usually simplified as "alienation," but that might be considered from another angle as the essential impulse toward privacy, for where but in privacy could the a new monstrous "I" come to terms with itself?

This new awareness—I realize now—more or less coincided with my reading the novel. It was most likely my attitude that made Holden so

attractive to me, and the exposure to Holden that quickly refined the edge
on my attitude. However the chicken-egg dynamic worked, from that
time on, my secret sense of difference, of being misunderstood and subject to the self-serving "phony" machinations of adults—all those things
that took on such emphasis in my life—are scored with his unmistak-
able voice.

I often think about reading and possession: reading as a way of inviting myself to be overtaken, commanded by another person's sense of
the world *and* reading as something one has, holds, and keeps. As owner-
ship. Certainly when I first read *Catcher* as a fourteen-year-old boy, both
were true. If I don't recall many of my specific reactions to scenes in
the novel, I do have a powerful deep-down memory of that voice—"If
you really want to hear about it"—circulating, jazzing through my system. And I *was* possessed. I couldn't shake the feeling off, couldn't not
hear the tone and thrust of Holden's judgments attaching themselves to
my own. Suddenly everything seemed to come toward me through the
strange wavy glass that was his take on things. At the same time, I felt the
intimate confidence of having something that was uniquely mine, a talisman, which was both the physical book, there to be opened and entered,
and—in some ways even better—the idea of the book. The inner world
of Holden as represented by that little paperback was my powerful secret.
No matter what was going on in my day, my life, I needed only to picture
that cover to feel a lift of secure well-being. I knew just where in physical
space to find the voice that anchored me to myself.

Catcher was Holden, Holden's voice, which caught as no other voice
ever has the unpredictable jumped-up inwardness of the fourteen-year-
old. What happened to that feeling, where did it go? It's a cliché, but
in fact we *do* forget what that time feels like. To the outside—adult—
world the teenager often looks alien, sullen and awkward, that's obvious
enough. But turn the lens around, remember how to the teenager, so recently still immersed in the matter-of-factness of childhood, what is alien
is the world, especially the unbearable conspiracy of grown-ups and what
is suddenly revealed to be a great system of delusions and hypocrisies.
This—the great lie of adulthood—is what undoes Holden; his response

sets him up as the martyr figure for the lost cause of childhood, the self-appointed protector of that innocence. Holden's beautiful fantasy is to position himself on the edge of the "crazy" cliff near where the thousands of children are playing, "to catch everybody if they start to go over the cliff"—but he cannot himself find a secure place to stand. For there is no secure place to stand, and this recognition brings on his breakdown even as, paradox of paradoxes, the voice that is registering that recognition is the sanest-sounding voice many of us hear in the miasma of our teenage disaffection.

The narrative is easy to sum up. Holden Caulfield, about to be expelled from his current boarding school, Pencey Prep—there have been other expulsions—leaves early and spends a few days by himself in New York City, before going to find his parents and take the consequences. There, he checks into a downtown hotel, takes an old girlfriend to a play, has a depressed, unconsummated interlude with a prostitute, gets drunk, visits an old teacher, and sneaks into his family's apartment to talk to his younger sister, Phoebe. He has no crises, really, and goes through no dramatic resolutions. And indeed, when I sometimes—it does happen—meet people who don't love the novel, who never felt that peculiar possessiveness about it, they will usually say that they got bored because nothing happened. It's true—if you take away the flow of Holden's voice, nothing does. Still, I have a hard time believing that anyone could start the novel and not be drawn in by the stunning comic pathos of its tone. More to the point, I can't imagine I would have anything much to say to a person who hadn't ever felt that terrible dissonance, that almost killing despair in the face of the betrayals required to gain entry through the gate marked "adulthood."

Once you grant that the voice is the thing, the alpha and omega, then it should just be a matter of pinning down what it is *about* the voice. Just. I've made enough stabs at it in the past to know that there is no getting there through analysis. Which is only fitting, when you think about it, since analysis is the standard operating procedure of the false world, the world of reasonable responses and planned action.

Voice . . . as I mean it here, voice is that over-and-above quality that certain writing has which allows it not only to transmit information or

opinion or whatever else it is that writing transmits, but which also convinces the reader that there is a single, unified—*living*—sensibility gener-
ating the words. Voice is the aura of writing, the sense of confidentiality;
it is what allows us to fall in with a writer, a narrator, and to succumb to
the illusion that we are being addressed. And in this respect, *Catcher* is a
tour de force. I can't think of a single moment in the book where I am
not directly in Holden's immediate intimate earshot, listening carefully.
The natural effect of this is the possessiveness I'm talking about. If I have
felt addressed, confided in, then I feel the book is uniquely mine. The author, the narrator, is *my* friend, the kind of person I could imagine calling
late at night on the phone.

A voice like Holden's compels our trust and identification, and his
status as a misfit-loner intensifies the bond. There are so many passages
that capture Holden's isolation, but the most nuanced and affecting ones
pinpoint not only his critical detachment, but also his ambivalence. It's
as if his anxious self-division puts the edge on his perceptions and makes
his discomfort seem more acute. Early in the novel, for instance—in the
first real scene—Holden goes to say good-bye to "old Spencer," his history teacher. He makes the visit out of a sense of personal duty—to honor
some feeling that is not even clear to him. We see as soon as he arrives
not only how Holden regards the man, but, far more important, how he
filters the general pathos of human situations, how he manages to fuse the
most pitiless clarity with a compensating indulgence:

> I just mean that I used to think about old Spencer quite a lot,
> and if you thought about him *too* much, you wondered what the
> heck he was still living for. I mean he was all stooped over, and
> he had very terrible posture, and in class, whenever he dropped a
> piece of chalk at the blackboard, some guy in the first row always
> had to get up and pick it up and hand it to him. That's awful, in
> my opinion. But if you thought about him just enough and not
> *too* much, you could figure it out that he wasn't doing too bad
> for himself. For instance, one Sunday when some other guys and
> I were over there for hot chocolate, he showed us this old beat-up

Navajo blanket that he and Mrs. Spencer'd bought off some Indian in Yellowstone Park. You could tell old Spencer'd got a big bang out of buying it. That's what I mean. You take somebody old as hell, like old Spencer, and they can get a big bang out of buying a blanket.

Holden *likes* Spencer, feels sorry for him even as it is the teacher who claims to be worried about his student. But Holden's essential fondness, and his sharply honed awareness for vulnerability and the pathos of vulnerability, does not undercut his less flattering responses:

> Then he said, "I had the privilege of meeting your mother and dad when they had their little chat with Dr. Thurmer some weeks ago. They're grand people."
>
> "Yes, they are. They're very nice."
>
> Grand. There's a word I really hate. It's a phony. I could puke every time I hear it.
>
> Then all of a sudden old Spencer looked like he had something very good, something sharp as a tack, to say to me. He sat up more in his chair and sort of moved around. It was a false alarm, though. All he did was lift the *Atlantic Monthly* off his lap and try to chuck it on the bed, next to me. He missed. It was only about two inches away, but he missed anyway. I got up and picked it up and put it down on the bed. All of a sudden then, I wanted to get the hell out of the room. I could feel a terrific lecture coming on. I didn't mind the idea so much, but I didn't feel like being lectured to and smell Vicks Nose Drops and look at old Spencer in his pajamas and bathrobe all at the same time. I really didn't.

The scene grows more excruciating as Spencer confronts Holden with his own exam paper, even reading select passages: "He put my goddam paper down then and looked at me like he'd just beaten hell out of me in ping-pong or something. I don't think I'll ever forgive him for reading me that crap out loud."

In this short scene we are exposed to much of the character's range—his hypervigilant eye, his core soft-heartedness, his awareness of himself as a tough case, and his aggrieved sense of honor. This is a young man strikingly at odds with himself, the aspects of his deeper nature continually shifting and jostling, offering him—and us—no place of equilibrium.

This impression is intensified when Holden goes back to his dorm, there meeting up with his roommate, the oafish jock Stradlater, and his unappealing pimple-squeezing neighbor, Ackley. To himself he makes the most devastating personal observations (about their hygiene, their insipid vanities) while keeping up an essentially comradely chatter. His poise is tested when Stradlater asks Holden to write an English paper for him while he goes out with a girl named Jane, Holden's old neighbor. Stradlater fancies himself as irresistible, a scorer, and Holden, who has great protective affection for Jane, can hardly bear to picture them together. Still, he agrees, and after his roommate leaves he sits down to work on the essay.

Faced with no assigned topic, Holden ends up writing about the baseball glove that used to belong to his younger brother, Allie. An innocent enough subject, we think, until we suddenly realize that Allie has died and that Holden is here opening the door on his most private pain. That he would write the piece for Stradlater seems masochistic in the extreme. But it also reveals just how much pressure the memory exerts. The whole situation is finally so excruciating for us to contemplate that when Stradlater later accuses him of getting the assignment wrong and Holden tears the thing up, we feel greatly relieved.

These inner struggles and contradictions help create the unique edge of Holden's voice and the tone of the novel. The voice is conversational and simple, exerting little or no stylistic flourish. It gains its artistic power by pulling us constantly toward the recognition of the very emotions it seems to be skirting through its colloquial offhandedness. We see this most clearly when Holden looks back on Allie's death. This is as straight-on as our narrator gets about the event that is probably the major cause of his breakdown:

> He never got mad at anybody. People with red hair are supposed
> to get mad very easily, but Allie never did, and he had very red
> hair. I'll tell you what kind of red hair he had. I started playing

golf when I was only ten years old. I remember once, the summer I was around twelve, teeing off and all, and having a hunch that if I turned around all of a sudden I'd see Allie. So I did, and sure enough, he was sitting on his bike outside the fence—there was this fence that went all around the course—and he was sitting there, about a hundred and fifty yards behind me, watching me tee off. That's the kind of red hair he had. God, he was a nice kid, though. He used to laugh so hard at something he thought of at the dinner table that he just about fell off his chair. I was only thirteen, and they were going to have me psychoanalyzed and all, because I broke all the windows in the garage. I don't blame them. I really don't. I slept in the garage the night he died, and I broke all the goddam windows with my fist, just for the hell of it. I even tried to break all the windows on the station wagon we had that summer, but my hand was already broken and everything by that time, and I couldn't do it. It was a very stupid thing to do, I'll admit, but I hardly didn't even know I was doing it, and you didn't know Allie. My hand still hurts me once in a while, when it rains and all, and I can't make a real fist any more—not a tight one, I mean—but outside of that I don't care much. I mean I'm not going to be a goddam surgeon or a violinist or anything *any*way.

The innocence and the put-on offhandedness of the tone combine with volatile effect. A whole psychology is laid bare for us.

ALLIE'S DEATH, a terrible trauma for Holden, has had the effect of making him hyperattuned to the forces that ambush and destroy the innocent. This vigilance expresses itself as a profound—and for the reader poignant—split, the one part of his being alert at every moment for the telltale hypocrisies of adults, the other fiercely protective of all that is yet uncorrupted. The hypocrisies, though they are often laughably small scale, are nevertheless all the evidence Holden needs that the fallen are not to be entrusted with the care of the unsuspecting young.

Throughout the novel we see how this split plays out. Scene after scene

is built around the tension, whether with "old Spencer," where both
hypocrisy and innocence are somehow located in one person, or with
Stradlater, whose sexual aggressiveness Holden perceives as a threat to
Jane; or later, as *Catcher* moves toward its culminating break, in Holden's
frenetic determination to cleanse the words "Fuck you" from the wall
of his sister Phoebe's old school (he has recently had a prostitute sent
to his room, by the way), and the outrage he feels when his old teacher,
Mr. Antonili, comes over in the dark to pat him when he is sleeping on
his couch. This last, especially, is an unacceptable violation—a conver-
sion of trust into threat—and it puts Holden right over the line. Walking
down the street a few hours later after he has fled from Antonili's apartment we see him nearly immobilized:

> Every time I came to the end of a block and stepped off the god-
> dam curb, I had this feeling that I'd never get to the other side of
> the street. I thought I'd just go down, down, down, and nobody'd
> ever see me again. Boy, did it scare me. You can't imagine. I started
> sweating like a bastard—my whole shirt and underwear and
> everything. Then I started doing something else. Every time I'd
> get to the end of a block I'd make believe I was talking to my
> brother Allie. I'd say to him, "Allie, don't let me disappear. Allie,
> don't let me disappear. Allie, don't let me disappear. Please,
> Allie." And then when I'd reach the other side of the street with-
> out disappearing, I'd *thank* him. Then it would start all over
> again as soon as I got to the next corner.

For Salinger, innocence is not simply an ideal uncorrupted condition—it
is also a protective, possibly even redemptive, force. To that end, we see,
Holden has internalized Allie, invested him with talismanic power, as if
he were the principle of innocence itself.

HOLDEN'S PANIC ATTACK leads directly to his decision to start hitchhiking west as soon as he has contacted his sister Phoebe. She is another
of Salinger's many precocious, prematurely wised-up children—at least so

we think when they have their late-night conversation in the family apartment. But when Phoebe later shows up at the museum to say good-bye, as they had arranged, he sees, as we see, that she is just a little girl lugging a big suitcase. She wants to come with him, and her manner is now imploring: "Can't I go with you? Holden? Can't I? *Please.*" But Holden can't bear that his little sister should in any way have to suffer his confusions. The only way he can find to buy her off is to take her to the Central Park Zoo, where, in the last real scene of the novel, he convinces her to ride the carrousel. Holden is by now desperate enough to lie; he violates his unstated but obvious code of honesty by promising Phoebe that he won't be leaving after all. Tense as the situation is, this next-to-last chapter finds a joyous closure. I find it very hard not to see Phoebe through Holden's eyes as suspended in a perpetual childhood—so long as the music lasts:

> Boy, it began to rain like a bastard. In *buckets,* I swear to God. All
> the parents and mothers and everybody went over and stood right
> under the roof of the carrousel, so they wouldn't get soaked to
> the skin or anything, but I stuck around on the bench for quite a
> while. I got pretty soaking wet, especially my neck and my pants.
> My hunting hat really gave me quite a lot of protection, in a way,
> but I got soaked anyway. I didn't care, though. I felt so damn
> happy all of a sudden, the way old Phoebe kept going around and
> around. I was damn near bawling, I felt so damn happy, if you
> want to know the truth. I don't know why. It was just that she
> looked so damn *nice,* the way she kept going around and around,
> in her blue coat and all. God, I wish you could've been there.

The final chapter, three paragraphs long, closes the narrative circle. "That's all I'm going to tell about," says Holden, reminding us of the opening: "If you really want to hear about it—" We learn that he just "got sick," that he has been put in a hospital or facility of some sort, that his older brother D. B., a once-fine writer who has sold out, who has become a literary "prostitute" in Hollywood, visits him there. Holden's last words—fond and reconciling—are about missing everybody he has known, "Even old Stradlater and Ackley. . . ."

I suggested at the beginning that *Catcher in the Rye* had a great deal to do with the formation of the 1960s counterculture sensibility. This is the kind of influence that can't be proved, and to some it will even seem nonsensical. Holden was in no way political; he advocated nothing. Neither was he any sort of hippie in the bud, unless we count his fantasy near the end of leaving New York and setting himself up in a cabin somewhere away from the world. But even this seems more like a projection of Salinger's own desire for isolation; there is no spiritual or philosophical program attached. Yet I would still say: ask any member of that great white demographic (I don't know if he had any pervasive influence on black or Hispanic teens) about their deep formation, what helped push them to reject the status quo and embrace a new way of things, and along with Bob Dylan and the Beatles you will hear Salinger's name.

No question, Holden Caulfield was deeply implicated in the birth of attitude in American youth culture. He made it cool to be outside, critical of the whole show. He gave us the tone we needed and showed us the right gestures to make; he did as much as a literary character could to make an honest response to things attractive. But that special chemistry of influence didn't happen overnight. Don't forget, the novel was published at the beginning of the 1950s, and though it had a young readership from the start, it didn't become a generational bible for many years. The times weren't yet ready. By which I mean that Holden's visions of the traitorous hypocrisy of adults, however accurate psychologically, didn't yet map to a broadly perceived cultural split. It took issues like civil rights and Vietnam to make the generational gulf fully obvious. But as soon as that happened—when the escalating woes of our society were seen to grow from the beliefs and actions of the society of elders (Johnson, Nixon, MacNamara, et al)—the stance made perfect sense: no one over thirty was to be trusted.

That sharp polarizing of values came quickly. For me, I know, it happened in a matter of a few months, over the summer of 1968, with the assassinations of Robert Kennedy and Martin Luther King and the billy-club police fascism at the Chicago Democratic Convention. A whole new weather system had muscled in. The terms of the opposition were seen to be absolute, and to speak out was suddenly imperative. Against the fallen world of our fathers, we proposed a counterworld—innocent, integrated, noncapitalistic, noncompetitive. Where ideas and philosophies ran short, we caulked things together with the rhetoric of our music and poetry. "Christ climbed down / from His bare Tree—" wrote Lawrence Ferlinghetti, and the indictment of commercialized spirit was not to be argued against. "I saw the best minds of my generation destroyed by madness," wrote Allen Ginsberg. And there was Dylan with his thousand quotable lines. It all seemed logical enough to us. We didn't understand that the truth of sentiment would not see us all the way through, that the world was hard and violent and would not yield to desire. It took us a long time to grasp this and a long time to make the correction. Although the hippie dream was only briefly iridescent at the very end of that decade, it lived on for some years after in the hearts of those who couldn't quite let it go.

This is where Holden figures in as a suffering patron saint. For the pain he registered in his own life—the phonies at Pencey Prep (and everywhere else in the world), the unbearable vulnerability of innocence—was suddenly writ large in the culture. It mapped out the same tension-split between what we saw as the mendacious adults presiding over our fates and that version of innocence which has, in retrospect, come to seem like the most heartbreaking folly. Did we really believe in our deeper hearts that we were going to establish a peace-loving and cooperative alternative culture? I wonder where we found this fairy-dust credulity and whether any other generation in history has embraced so fully a utopian fantasy.

The only way I can try to account is by looking back to my own remembered experience. My short-form explanation is that as a generation we experienced a historical first—a collective self-recognition made possible by the convergence of music and television. We were all together for a one-time flashbulb moment that happened in 1968, with the televised protests at the Democratic Convention; millions upon millions of us, primed already by years of pop-culture saturation, suddenly "got" that not only were we profoundly different from "them," but that we were an exciting *historical* force. Connecting this recognition with the disengaged gentleness of the newly bourgeoning hippie subculture is harder. There was the banner of hair, of course, as well as the shared secrecy of drugs, the engulfing tide of music, the festivals. Taken one by one these are merely relevant phenomena. Taken together and shaken they created an atmosphere, a pervasive national mood that was hard to ignore then and remains, for some of us, nostalgically encoded in certain songs of the time.

The mood, the fever, was real, I swear to it, and it moved through the culture like a contagion. For two or more years after the summer of 1968 we lived inside what Geoffrey O'Brien christened "dream time," an adrenaline adventure forever marked off from what came before. For some this was about drugs, but even nondruggies testified to the difference. There was a changed sense of futurity—instead of the known, expected, planned-for thing, we felt the chaotic thrill of the unknown. No one knew what was going to happen next. Life—the world—was an open game, in progress, with everything riding on the throw of the dice. Everything we had assumed and come to dread was there to be gotten rid of, changed. Then, for many reasons, because it is the way of things, the feeling went away, abruptly and terribly. And when it did—it was gone by the middle of 1971—it was not to be called back. Political zeal collapsed, communes faltered, drugs took their inevitable, long-awaited toll, and the life went out of our music. Back there, left behind as fond commemoratives, were the rallying songs, the pundits, the books and poems that had meant so much—"Howl," *One Flew Over the Cuckoo's Nest, The Catcher in the Rye* . . .

PERSONAL DECADES WENT BY—a whole vast chunk of time swallowed by work, parenting, and trying at adulthood—before *Catcher* signaled to me again. I had not even picked it up to look at, that's how dated, beside the point, and sad it seemed. All bound up with the dream that had leaked away, it was too obviously a reminder of the rawness of being young, as was Jack Kerouac, and, for a very long time, all of the folk music I had once listened to so obsessively. But a few years back, that changed again, though now it was not the culture, it was just me. For whatever reason, I was different inside, more ready and willing to tune in again. If you leave certain ideas and feelings alone for long enough, they sometimes renew their appeal; they become interesting again for other reasons. This time I was a father with young children, a teacher with students who only got younger every year, a grown man who had started to spin with trite predictability back to thoughts and desires long in abeyance. I wanted something from my younger self, I don't even know what. But finally there came the day when I picked *Catcher* up again, and as soon as I did it happened: I fell in with that perfect enduring cadence, the universal note of adolescent disaffection: "If you really want to hear about it . . ." And though the gap was wide, the spark crossed with a sweet reliability. It was surprisingly easy suddenly to find Holden again.

SOMEWHERE IN THIS SAME PERIOD—my late-forties—I started waking early. Most mornings I would be awake and alert by 5:30 and lying in bed was not an option. So I began my ritual of walking the streets. In every season, weather-permitting, I would finish off my coffee and set out into the neighborhood for an hour or so. It became a time to think, sketch out the day, and apply the rhythms of strenuous hiking to whatever thought-obsession was current. At first I went alone. But then, a few years back, when she was twelve or thirteen, my daughter Mara began to insist that I take her along. Now it's the two of us. Most every morning, no matter the season, I flick on her bedroom light before 6:00 a.m. and say, "I'm walking—"

Father and daughter. People are amazed when I tell them what we do. "How wonderful!" They imagine us talking, bonding. But in fact most of the time we just push along, some yards apart, thinking our own thoughts. We can go for two or three miles with only the sound of our walking between us. It *is* wonderful.

Every so often, though—who knows why?—we will get going on something. She will tell me about a dream she had, or start talking about a friend, or we'll talk about school, or music, or something she's reading. It was during one of these conversations that we made our Holden connection. I had noticed with surprise that she had my old Signet copy of *Catcher* on her desk, and I asked her about it. She gave me a sharp, interested look. "I read it all in one day," she said. "I loved it!" Just like that we entered the phase of Holden. There was no sense to it, no structure or method or big literary dialogue, nothing but a repeated invoking of the book between us. It lasted for weeks. "Well, Dad," she'd say, talking about something else, "as old Holden would put it—" or certain phrases would come creeping in, how her English teacher spent the whole period "just slingin' the ol' bull," or else, apropos of nothing that had been said, one or the other of us would come out with, "I love that part where—" bringing up the scene with the nuns, or Ackley, or Holden riding on the bus with the headmaster's daughter or how he let down the whole fencing team. The point was somehow just to connect, to leap over the opening divide while we still could, to call up that implicit us/them picture of things, which of course made perfect sense for my daughter, and was the logic of her world, but was a bit stranger for me to pretend to now that I was at least technically well along on the path to being one of *them*. But at those moments, more clearly than at other times, I would feel the relief of being back where I belonged, inwardly squared off against the two-faced fools who felt they had to watch over the system of *shoulds* and *oughts* without which the world couldn't possibly function. And from these talks I realized that the secret of Holden, his undying appeal, is that he remains fixed, through the genius of his disaffection, through Salinger's perfect grasp of the pathos of adolescence—its pained awareness of imminent fall—right at the point of sacrifice. Unable to take the one small required step toward accommodation, he becomes a martyr to the cause of doomed innocence, possessor of a cynicism that is so heartbreaking because it is entirely preemptive, in training for the disappointments of the life to come.

Love's Wound, Love's Salve

Knut Hamsun's *Pan*

———————————•———————————

WHEN I WAS A BOY growing up in Michigan, my mother was the great reader in the family, and my father, though deeply creative in his professional life, did not read at all. I worked out a big part of my Oedipal conflict, if that's what it was, by becoming a consumer of books myself. I looked to find my way to my mother's affections by heeding her signals; I turned to the authors she loved—at least those I could read—and soaked up whatever approval came my way. I imagined I saw my father scowling in the background.

My mother not only read—daily and with steady fixation—but she also spoke with open reverence about writers, relishing the sound of their names and book titles and the bits of lore she gleaned from the biographies she was always devouring. I knew about Hemingway and Hadley, Scott and Zelda, and Isak Dinesen and her coffee plantation long before I'd read any of these writers myself. All the news, however, came to me in the home language, Latvian, so that my own encounters with these authors—Ernest Hemingway, or Thomas Wolfe, or W. Somerset Maugham, or Jack London—always carried a tinge of strangeness laid over the base of familiarity.

The effect of my mother's devotion, apart from the pleasure of finding transport to all kinds of lit-up other places, was to impress on me the idea that there was nothing finer, worthier, than reading, except, of course, the writing that made reading possible.

While my mother loved a great many books and writers, she reserved a special reverence—so it seemed to me—for a handful of authors from her youth in Riga, especially those that had been published in a Pleiades-like series called Lielie Ziemelnieki (Great Northerners), all issued, as she described many times, in handsome, uniform bindings: Sigrid Undset, Selma Lagerlöf, but above all others, Knut Hamsun, his *Hunger, Mysteries, Victoria,* and *Pan,* those works of desperate lyrical romanticism.

I offer this little prologue to help explain why my encounter in late adolescence with *Pan* should have seemed so intense, so intended. True, it is one of the most heart-wrenching novels ever written. But in my mind I was not just reading a novel; I was also somehow making inroads on what I imagined was my mother's secret inner terrain. I was finding a connection to a world that predated me; in the process, I was putting down the first fragile roots of my own private life.

WE ALL KNOW that there can be special charged encounters between readers and books, when the whole experience is like a ready tinder going up at the touch of a flame—the tinder being the psychological susceptibility of the person holding the book and the flame being the intensity of a writer's particular vision. The image gets something of the feel of my original experience with this most harrowing of Hamsun's early works. For *Pan,* published when its author was still in his thirties, is a numbingly pure distillation of a young man's passion, of emotion unchecked by the rationalizations and deferrals that experience teaches.

As it happens, I read this little novel in the depths of my own most lovelorn summer. I was sixteen and secretly and clumsily in love with a girl named Kathleen. Tall, blond, dreamily beautiful, Kathleen was two classes behind me, very nearly still a girl, though she also had the disconcerting poise you sometimes find in those to whom life has been unaccountably generous. Beautiful people, I've noticed, often seem distant from themselves, slightly shocked, as if they can't quite believe what the mirror is sending back. For my part, I avoided reflective surfaces as much as possible, dreading the disconcerting trick they kept playing on me. The oaf who surprised me there had nothing to do with the fine-featured and poetic self I was nurturing.

I hid my passion, I had to, for it would have chased Kathleen away, and I couldn't imagine not being able to be near her. Kathleen—this was clear—saw herself as my friend, my companion in reverie, a fellow seeker. She liked it when I talked about lives as fates, or Zen (I knew nothing about Zen), or about the novels of Herman Hesse. On summer nights, after a long unromantic day stacking boxes in a candy warehouse, I would drive to Cranbrook, where I went to school and where her father was the dean of students, and she and I would walk around the grounds, circling Kingswood Lake in the deepening twilight. At every second I was aware of the nearness of her bright bare arms, the sway of her long hair, the little modulations of her tone when she laughed at my jokes. I imagined my fingers all over that skin, as any boy in my place would have done, but I didn't dare even the slightest nudge in her direction. Later, though, driving home down Lone Pine Road, windows open to the night, or replaying every step of our walk in my stark and stuffy little room, I wanted to cry out, to bark like a dog.

IT WAS IN THIS STATE that I first read—gulped down—Hamsun's novel, and when I did I was thrown down into a sadness from which it seemed there was no return, that felt, suddenly, like my first earned wisdom, confirmation of the fact that life touched by the genius of love was ultimately not to be endured. Although the situations were as different as could be, everything about that story and mine swirled together—I convinced myself that Hamsun had some mysterious access to my inner life. He gave me a language for thinking about my feelings for Kathleen.

Hamsun opens the novel with the account—seemingly innocent, contemplative, transparent—of one Lieutenant Glahn, who would have us believe he is just passing the time setting down a few recollected episodes from a summer that has already taken on the character of a dream:

These last few days I have thought and thought of the Nordland
summer's endless day. I sit here and think of it, and of a hut I
lived in, and of the forest behind the hut; and I have taken to
writing about it, just for my own amusement and to while away

the time. Time drags; it does not pass as quickly as I should like, although I have no cares and lead the gayest of lives. I am perfectly content with everything, and thirty is no great age. A few days ago I received a couple of bird's feathers from far away, from one who need not have sent them; just two green feathers folded in a sheet of paper with a coronet on it and fastened with a seal. It amused me to see two so fiendishly green feathers. Otherwise there is nothing to trouble me except a touch of arthritis now and then in my left foot, the result of an old shot wound that healed up long ago.

I remember that time went much faster two years ago, incomparably faster than now; the summer was gone before I realised it. It was two years ago, in 1855—I want to write about it to amuse myself—that something happened to me: or else I dreamt it.

Glahn tries to pass himself off as a man at peace, but even an unsophisticated reader, which I surely was in that long ago summer of 1968, has to grasp that these are the bravely bitter posturings of a man looking to master his pain. Phrases like "for my own amusement" and "although I have no cares" are standard-issue denials; but just in case we don't pick this up, there is the protruding giveaway "Otherwise there is nothing to trouble me," confirming that receiving those two green feathers was not an unalloyed pleasure. The power of *Pan* lies in how the gradually revealed emotional lacerations first contradict Glahn's adopted pose, and then undo him completely, to the point where effects have completely overwhelmed their causes.

THE OUTER CONTOUR of Glahn's summer, the slight and dreamy stuff of the plot, is easily sketched in. Glahn is, by temperament, one of life's great romantic solitaries. Taking a break from the larger world, living in a forest hut near a small Norwegian trading village, he passes the season alone, with only his beloved dog Aesop for company. When he is hungry, he hunts. Otherwise, he whiles away the endless hours daydreaming in his hut or wandering about in the forest, communing with nature in fugues of such pantheistic intensity that at times we think he will just merge with the great green Other: "Over by the edge of the forest there is fern and monk's hood, the heather is in bloom and I love its small flowers. I thank God for every heather flower I have ever seen; they have been like tiny roses on my path and I weep for love of them."

Cranbrook, though groomed and domesticated, was my slice of pastoral. Even before meeting Kathleen, I spent as much time as I could roaming the grounds—trailing along the artfully devised paths, sitting by the picturesque boathouse and gazing out over Kingswood Lake, where swans paddled in conventional pairs, or hunkered in one of my hillside spots with my notebook on my knees, looking for words that would somehow map those feelings which now seem so embarrassingly precious, but then were the finest thing in my life.

For Glahn it can't last, this perfect peace, this ecstatic natural concord. Into Eden comes Eve, in the form of Edvarda, the young daughter of Herr Mack, owner of the village trading post. She appears at Glahn's hut one day in the company of the stolidly pretentious man called simply the Doctor. He and Edvarda have been out walking and have decided to pay a call on Glahn.

The three talk awkwardly, moving from subject to subject, and it is only when the visitors have left that we are allowed to grasp the intense fixity with which Glahn has been regarding Edvarda: "Suddenly I saw before me her brown face and brown neck. She had tied her apron low on her hips to accentuate the length of her body, as was fashionable. Her thumb had a chaste and girlish look about it that touched me; and the few wrinkles on her knuckles were full of kindliness. She had a generous mouth, and her lips were red." Hardly the fruit of idle observation. These details have been gathered by an avid soul, the same soul that goes casting abroad in the forest for intimations of some higher connectedness.

THE ATTRACTION—and this marked a major divergence from my own story—turns out to be mutual. Thereupon, in keeping with the ancient principle of romantic magnetism, active whenever two people think only of each other, Glahn and Edvarda are soon running into each other everywhere—on the forest paths, down in the village. Here is the pure intoxication of young love, and if the particulars vary slightly across the surface, deep down they are subject to the delicious lifts and plunges of the universal erotic dance:

'You are happy to-day, you are singing,' she says, and her eyes sparkle.

'Yes, I am happy,' I answer. 'You have a smudge of something on your shoulder there, it's dust, from the road perhaps. I want to kiss it—no, please let me kiss it! Everything about you arouses tenderness in me, I am quite distracted by you. I didn't sleep last night.'

And that was quite true; for more than one night I had lain sleepless.

Edvarda takes the first initiative. She comes to Glahn's hut and, announcing her passion, stays the night; she plants the barb of the hook so that it will never be extricated.

The congruence, the easy romance, is soon—though we don't know why—pushed terribly awry. Glahn catches the first intimation: "Sometimes there would be a night when Edvarda stayed away; once she stayed away for two nights. Two nights. There was nothing wrong, and yet I had the feeling that my happiness has passed its peak." Whether this is an illustration of what Marcel Proust called "the intermittencies of love"—as if affection were a flame that must rise and fall—or just something perverse in the deep-down nature of things, some fateful coupling of eros and sadism, the idyllic romance of Glahn and Edvarda changes track almost as soon as it has begun.

WHAT FOLLOWS NOW is the kind of obsessive combat of the wills that D. H. Lawrence captured so accurately in his novels. Edvarda pulls away; Glahn suffers, sulks, practices feints of indifference. Then, just when he is strengthening toward a new resolve, ready to cut her loose, Edvarda flashes the ray of her vulnerable sweetness and Glahn is drawn back into the circuit, wanting and hoping.

Deeply drawn in myself, I was aware that behind the similarities—the profound bond I felt—were decisive differences. To start with, I was an innocent in all matters erotic, having by that point in my life done no more than kiss a girl, and that some years before. Whatever Glahn and Edvarda were up to in Glahn's hut was a simmering supposition. I had not so much as bent toward Kathleen to risk the unimaginable touch of lips. I had to use all of my imagination to compute the urgency of their inter-actions, and even then I'm sure I failed. On the other hand, the push-pull dynamic—I have heard it called the "rubber-band" effect—was already familiar, all the stratagems of withdrawal I tried to implement, and the aching scramble that came when Kathleen did the same. More than any-thing else, this crazy refusal of even a moment's equilibrium captured me.

AT ONE POINT, sitting near Glahn on a group outing to a nearby island, Edvarda admires the beautiful feathers he uses for tying flies. Glahn right away gives her two. "Please take them," he says, "let them be a memento." But a short time later, when they are returning in a rowboat together, Glahn seizes Edvarda's shoe and flings it far out over the water. He does not begin to understand his own impulse. But to the reader it feels exactly right: the air between them is crackling with disturbance.

SO THINGS CONTINUE for a time—sightings, meetings, rebuffs, spasms of searing jealousy whenever Glahn sees Edvarda giving her attention to another. The tension pushes them apart. Edvarda no longer comes to the hut at night. Glahn wanders about, miserable, but all obvious emotion is thrust below the waterline; he gives away none of his feelings when they chance to meet. As readers, though, we need no compass. We can reckon the state of his heart from his erratic actions, his distractedness. He throws himself into an affair with another village girl, but it just makes things worse. Nothing avails. Glahn's erotic grief has no way to discharge itself, and as it builds he is driven ever more irretrievably into himself.

Weeks then pass without encounter; summer is slowly winding down. As the time for Glahn's departure approaches, the pressure of his longing and frustration grows almost intolerable for the reader. As with any nar-rative of star-crossed love, we pit our own hopes against what we sense is the impossibility of the situation. It is the golden rule of all narrative art: the principle of wish fulfillment is stronger than the principle of common sense.

Just days before he must go, Glahn unexpectedly meets Edvarda at the counter of the village store:

> I greeted her, and she looked up but did not answer. Then it occurred to me that I did not want to ask for bread while she was there; I turned to the assistants and asked for powder and shot. While these were being weighed I kept my eye on her.
>
> A grey dress, much too small for her, its buttonholes worn; her flat breast heaved desperately. How she had grown during the summer! Her brow was pensive, those strange arched eyebrows were set in her face like two riddles, all her movements had become more mature. I looked at her hands, the expression in her long, delicate fingers affected me powerfully and made me tremble.

Then, on the day of his departure, almost as an afterthought—so he portrays it—Glahn decides he that he has to say farewell to Edvarda. He finds her at home, sitting with a book. His news seems to startle her, though we pick up but the slightest hint:

> 'Glahn, are you going away? Now?'
> 'As soon as the ship comes.' I seize her hand, both her hands, a senseless rapture takes possession of me and I burst out: 'Edvarda!' and stare at her.
>
> And in an instant she is cold, cold and defiant.

Edvarda can only say: "To think you are leaving already." A moment later she adds: "Who will come next year, I wonder?" At which point she seats herself with her book. The interview is over.

> But no—suddenly, perversely, she rises to her feet again with a parting request.

'I should like something to remind me of you when you have gone,' she said. 'There was something I thought of asking you for, but perhaps it is too much. Will you give me Aesop?'

Without reflecting I answered 'Yes'.

Later, alone in his hut, Glahn agonizes over his decision:

Why had she asked me to come and bring the dog myself? Did she want to talk to me, tell me something for the last time? I had nothing more to hope for. And how would she treat Aesop? Aesop, Aesop, she will torment you! Because of me she will whip you, caress you too perhaps, but certainly whip you in and out of season and utterly destroy you. . . .

I called Aesop, patted him, put our two heads together and reached for my gun. He was already whining with pleasure, thinking we were going out hunting. Again I put our two heads together, placed the muzzle of the gun against Aesop's neck and fired.

I hired a man to carry Aesop's body to Edvarda.

So much for Glahn's coy disingenuousness: "It amused me to see two so fiendishly green feathers." Indeed. I don't know that Nordic stoicism has ever showed itself more starkly, or the blade of unrequited love ever turned quite so painfully in its wound. When I read these words I was in the grip, so I imagined, of my hopeless passion. Not only did I identify my own feelings, but the novel stirred me up, made everything excruciating, hyper-conscious. Kathleen, so shy to begin with, would get perceptibly more aloof whenever I inched myself the closer to risking some admission—she had a woman's radar. But now I understood; Hamsun had given me the hard news about love. And about life—for in the wake of such complete devastation I saw no point in anything. I took that sadness down into the center of my heartsick summer and incubated it there.

PAN CONCLUDES with a section called "Glahn's Death: A paper from the year 1861." Six years later, in other words. The short section comes to us in the voice of a bitter comrade of Glahn's ("But Thomas Glahn had his faults, and I am not disposed to conceal them, since I hate him."), a man who first met the lieutenant two years earlier somewhere in India or Ceylon. The gist of the "paper"—a confession, or self-exoneration, of sorts—is that the strange, erratic Glahn, after befriending him, set about systematically goading him, to the point where the man had no choice but to act. And one day when they were out hunting he did act:

> The court entered his name and the circumstances of his death in a stitched and bound register, and in that register is written that he is dead, I tell you, yes, and even that he was killed by a stray bullet.

How can we ever measure the effects of a work like this on a susceptible young reader? I was shaken to the core. I was just sixteen; I had no wisdom to hold against this vision of hopelessness, no mitigating perspective. There was nothing but the riot of my own emotions, the overblown certainty that if Kathleen did not recognize and greet my feeling I would have nothing to get me through my life. At that point the only thing that cut against my despair was my hope. We were still seeing each other, walking and talking, visiting with her best friend Vicky; she was still hearing out my thoughts and confidences. Somehow I would bring her to see who I was, how I felt about her.

I never did. Kathleen announced one day in late July that she was going away for a month with her family. She left a day later. I swallowed the sudden fact of her absence like some horrid medicine—I had no choice—and I resolved to wait. While she was gone I did everything I could to make myself into the person she would want to be with. As never before or since in my life, I exerted desperate discipline. I determined to merge with my poetical inner man—to become lean and intent. For long weeks I held myself to cereal and yogurt; I shirked family meals and fought the gnawing pain with long walks. If I am nostalgic for anything now it's that uncorrupted intensity. It worked. Day by day I lost weight. I got so I could bear to stand in the upstairs bathroom and stare at myself. I *liked* the dangerous person I saw there. Time passed—hot, obsessed weeks. I lay in my bed at night and listened to Leonard Cohen, my mystery man. I whittled at my soul until I had made it worthy.

AND THEN the strangest thing happened. I grew, altered, finished out something in myself so that there was no going back. I can't explain it, but when summer ended and Kathleen finally came back, everything was different. Time had worked its decisive will: all that relentless focus had miraculously moved me away from wanting her. When school started a few weeks later, someone else appeared in my life and I gave everything I had hoarded to her instead. When I did see Kathleen from time to time—was I imagining this?—she was beaming a new kind of light in my direction. But I was no longer susceptible.

STILL, I COULDN'T LOOK AT *Pan* for many years. It compressed so much of my pain and my original longing in its pages, and even the receding memory was a threat. So much of my young man's unhappiness was stored away there. I remember having the superstitious feeling that if I were to open the cover and glance at the words I would come undone. So the book was put away, and when I went away to college, moving my prize possessions, mainly books and records, I didn't bring it with me.

But books—or the emotions we have secreted there—have a way of exerting influence even as we imagine we have left them far behind. Like opportunistic growing things, they find out our unguarded places, the little crevices in our daydreaming selves, and then they surface—as memories, or just by adding their distinct tone to certain moods and imaginings.

Pan was such a book—in itself, but also through what it activated, how it played on deeper parts of my nature. Origins are about a good deal more than speech and manners. They announce themselves through disposition, affinities and biases—essential ways of being that seem lie to far below the accidents of personality and absorbed culture. I knew none of this then, but over time, and very gradually, I've had to recognize that I pull toward certain obviously Northern things—images, natural settings, people, styles of behavior. I am powerfully affected by landscapes of pine and birch and compelled by certain kinds of Scandinavian faces.

Moreover, try as I might I can't make myself into the kind of impulsive, declarative person I so admire, what I have typecast to myself as the explosive Sicilian. No, I recognize in myself the Hamlet disposition, everything always "sicklied o'er with the pale cast of thought." I am, like my people, reticent, melancholic, solitary, most comfortable with emotional understatement—"repressed" would be the term *du jour*. My eye has never been drawn by posters for tropical vacation spots or crowded Mardi Gras extravaganzas. I need my dark wooded paths and bracingly harsh climates.

This slowly emerging recognition of temperament may help to explain how it was that *Pan* slowly drew me back. I'd marked the book as painful and left it with my other souvenirs of growing up. But I never got rid of it. Year after year I spotted it on bookstore shelves, or in libraries, and each time I did I'd feel a small confirming tug, a light touch of recognition. It was more than a book I'd read, a sad story I knew. Those covers also held pressed between them a strong atmospheric recollection. I find it hard to particularize. The book held the feeling of so many things—those woody paths, the shore, the cold gray water, the awkward way people carried themselves when they met, those explosions of recklessness, the layers and layers of privacy. I suppose I knew I would have to return to it, in spite of all my deep reluctance.

I FINALLY GAVE IN and bought a secondhand paperback and began to read. Although it was a complicated, inwardly contested decision, I felt I was ready. Enough time had passed. I was sure that I would finally prevail over the romanticism; that Glahn's introverted stoicism would now strike me as forced; that his pure-hearted communings with nature would seem overheated. I was armed against it.

And utterly powerless. For such is the power of a book, a memory, that it can in a flash outwit any structure or system we have raised against it. True, I had steeled myself against Glahn, against the sadness of his story, against his complete destruction by the passion that had reared up in his unguarded heart. But I hadn't braced against the encounter with myself, the sixteen-year-old who went at the world, at the mirage ideal of love, with such unscreened intensity. I read *Pan,* but the person I kept meeting on those woodland paths was my untutored younger self. I felt heartache from the first sentence on, a hurt so sweet and piercing that it was hard to turn the pages. Worse, though—for sorrow recollected can also bring a certain pleasure—was my self-reproach. As I read I indicted myself: I had, in stages, without ever planning it, traded off that raw nerved-up avidness. I'd had to, of course; it was inevitable. We don't survive the dream of love, not at that pitch. We build in our safeguards and protective reflexes—we cultivate cynicism. We give in to the repetitions, let them gradually tame the erratic element. We grow wise and balance—or perish. Still, to encounter the ghost of that self here, now, in full adulthood, was a shock.

BUT I HAVE PARRIED IT. I one day found the rationale, the way to understand, and when it came to me I felt a great rush of relief. "This is not the tragic truth of things." I very nearly said the words out loud. I remember. I was in a distressed state walking along a scenic path in the woods of Vermont, just a few years ago. I felt the uproar of the midlife demons, and then the surfacing of the old deadly question. Did love have to issue in torment, did it have to fail?

AND THEN I HAD a thought about this book, a thought so clear it was like an answer to my question, a balm for my wound. What Hamsun offered was not the final truth, I realized, because whatever *Pan* told about love, it somehow left out the people who do the loving. I hadn't been able to see that before, that the book is the legend of desire feasting upon itself, struggling against itself, turning on itself to get rid of the unbearable pain, the source of all wanting. Glahn and Edvarda were just figures in the dance. They had nothing to hold up against the pulverizing momentum in their separate souls. They had, I saw it now, no . . . relationship. There had been, for all the beauty of the summer nights, all the mystery, no person "Glahn" and no person "Edvarda," only a crazy fever of wanting and a despair of not-having. The novel was a pure expression of youth, which loves crazily, without resource, without the encumbrances that are also finally the fuel of real love. Realizing this saved me from the harshest effects of my sadness, allowed me to close the book up around the beautiful black feather I found one day and that I keep as a bookmark; it allowed me my equanimity, which is now punctured, but not riddled by, secret doubts.

"I Don't Believe That"

D. H. Lawrence's *Women in Love*

I

T'S HARD NOW, all these years later, for me to repossess my sense of D. H. Lawrence. I recently finished a weeklong immersion in *Women in Love* and found it heated-up and involving in ways that felt immediately familiar, never mind the fact that it's been thirty years since I last read the book. But it feels difficult, almost impossible, to reenter that larger thing, the feeling of the world—of life—as Lawrence once gave it to us.

I say "us" because since taking on the novel again I've brought up Lawrence's name with a number of my near-contemporaries—all of them readers, if not writers—and they have, without exception, corroborated me, confiding (sometimes sheepishly) that he is a writer with whom they have deep, complicated associations and who represents something more than the sum of his books. For them, too, Lawrence stands for a way of looking, a way of living, and a cultural atmosphere that has vaporized so completely that we can only shake our heads, puzzling over whether it ever existed at all.

This, as much as any specific interest in the work, is what originally sent me back to *Women in Love*. I wanted to see if anything in the prose could trigger me, return me to some of the intensity of being seventeen or eighteen and for the first time really up against the great unknowns of existence. The gambit worked. The novel did indeed get me back, but it was not via the rapid transport of revelation, or through some sudden overwhelming wash of sensation. I got there confusedly, in stages, with all sorts of sidelong deflections, all of which are, of course, relevant not just to Lawrence but to the deeper itineraries of reading.

I FOUND MY WAY to Lawrence first by hearsay, through a complex of associations that had more to do with my private romantic meanderings than anything overtly literary. I was sixteen years old and finishing up my junior year at Cranbrook, a private school outside Detroit that I attended as a day student. Since my transfer that fall I'd been living out the angst of the shy outsider, the new boy who could not find a way to break in, moping about the beautifully landscaped grounds in a state of hyperalienated self-consciousness. The first human being to have gotten the joke, to have seen existence for what it really is, I tried to face up to my inevitable life-long solitude. But for all my philosophical conviction, I hadn't quite ruled out real love yet—my rebellious daydreams were still scripting unexpected encounters with pensive beauties.

Into this bog of vanities arrived my first new friends and after that, in sequence, the name, the idea, and then the work of Lawrence. Indeed, one of the many reflective meditations to be written alongside those that study the role of reading in self-formation, would explore just how we find our way to the important authors of our lives; it would pay special attention to the instigating role played by fantasy.

Here, before anything, I have to credit the influence of Victoria— Vicky—Swain, who was a year younger than I was but who dramatized in every way the old truism about girls maturing faster than boys. Vicky was a sophomore at Kingswood, Cranbrook's sister school, and she was best friends with the beautiful Kathleen, for whom I pined with a first-timer's intensity, so it was in part out of base opportunism that I cultivated her. I was a complete social amateur, but Vicky made the relationship ordeal seem effortless. Easygoing, socially irrepressible, talented at making everything I said seem witty and original, she promptly pulled me into a complexly confiding friendship. Where Kathleen was always cool and distracted, hovering like a mirage in a twilight vision, Vicky was the opposite. Within weeks of our meeting I was a familiar in her family's living room, trading jokes with her older brothers and discussing world issues with her parents.

As I got to know Vicky better, I realized to what extent she lived in a fantasy world of all things English. It was not just that she wore her long dark hair—"tresses"—in pre-Raphaelite disarray, or that she enjoyed making and serving tea, or that she manufactured just the slightest hint of an accent, it was that in her mind she seemed to move around in a romantic conjuring of English manor life. I don't know where this impulse originated—books and movies, I suppose (though this was before the era of *Masterpiece Theatre*)—but it was real, and retrospect confirms it. Years later Vicky married a man she had first met when he was an English exchange student at Cranbrook, and she has been living in England for the last thirty years. Even back then she was hard at work on her fate.

I can't remember how Vicky made the connection to Lawrence, or what book of his she read first, but I know the name and that one novel were suddenly very much in the air. And not just in Vicky's conversation. Two of my classmates, Mark Schwayder and Jim Rector—both, like me, susceptible to Vicky's energy and enthusiasm—were enlisted. Only they acquired leading parts in the great Lawrence show, and I for some reason did not.

The summer before my senior year was Lawrence-saturated, *Women in Love*–saturated, though I had not even read the thing. My relation to the work and writer, to this whole situation, might have been very different if I had picked up the novel right away. I might have preempted the long season of wondering; I probably wouldn't have created around Lawrence so enticing an aura or extended to Vicky, Mark, and Jim such a sense of privileged possession. Why didn't I just get in step? The book was so much around us, so *assumed*—with a few days' reading I could have joined the party. Now I would say that this is probably why I didn't. I have always been cursed with a resistant, contrarian nature. Offer me white, I'll choose black. If I hear that everyone is devouring a given novel, I tend to hurry in the opposite direction—no Lawrence for me. Never mind that the conversation of these three friends was now every other sentence Birkin this and Gudrun that. I kept myself at the outskirts.

But I was curious and alert nevertheless—fascinated. If Mark joked that Jim was at some moment "just like Gerald"—and everyone laughed—I

imagined a world of nuance, probably far more than was intended. In my
sharpened-up condition, hoarding details, remembering references even
when I didn't know what they were references *to,* I created a Lawrence who
in many ways exceeded his own remarkable self. Onto the image of the
bearded consumptive—I knew the face from posters and book covers—I
piled up the loftiest attributions. Here was the consummate psychologist
of relationships; here was the prophet of a liberated sexuality. Lawrence
was, as the title of one of his biographies had it, "the priest of love." And as
we know—all of us who at one time or another have idealized someone—
these projections are hard to shake off.

What I did was to "Prufrock" the event—I overprepared it. And when
I did, many months later, read *Women in Love,* I brought to it some of
that aura I'd manufactured. Whatever Lawrence had put on the page,
which of course was considerable, came filtered through the dense screen
of my expectations. I jumped in to find the story, the adventure, and it
seemed to be everything my friends had advertised. But memory is never
not temperamental. What I keep from that first reading turns out to be
less a narrative and more like a clutch of picture postcards, though truth
be told narrative is hardly ever the point with Lawrence. His interest is
in creating fields of energy, scenarios of competing wills and drives that
eventually expend themselves.

There is a basic situational premise. Two sisters, Ursula and Gudrun,
the grown daughters of a town schoolteacher, fall in love with two men,
Rupert (known to all as Birkin) and Gerald, who then befriend one another. As the sisters are different—Ursula meek if quietly willful, Gudrun
aggressive—so Birkin and Gerald come together from opposite sides of
the spectrum. Gerald is a mine owner's entitled son, a physical man with
obvious ambitions and drives; Birkin is a school inspector, a fiery free-
thinker determined to make sense of the world for himself. Following
the course of their myriad interactions, the novel becomes an epic of
subliminal negotiations, an elaborate anatomy of sexual power, most
of it carried on in long, discursive episodes. That much I knew when I
went back. But much else had shifted. Scenes I recollected as long and
involved were but a page or two, while others, faintly inscribed—like

Birkin and Gerald's early London interlude—stretched on and on with insidious intent.

In some ways the point is moot. When I focus in on my memories of this period—those that relate to reading Lawrence—what stands out most prominently is not the intensive dissecting of relationships, or what must even then have seemed like an emancipated treatment of desire and sexuality, but the lone figure of Rupert Birkin. For me, it was overwhelmingly Birkin's book. His presence caught and fixated me, and I allowed him to become one of my key figures, a very particular touchstone.

We too often simplify or even overlook the complicated and important dynamic of literary identification. It's not just that the reader claims affinities with a character or takes special interest in his fate or lives vicariously in fantasy with him (or her). These things happen, of course, but they don't, even all together, explain away the involvement. I would argue that in certain cases—especially with the books that prove truly transformational—readers internalize the vital characters in some of the same ways that they incorporate the presence (and influence) of real people. This may sound facile and exaggerated, but it deserves attention. Although the character doesn't really "exist," he or she is a being imbued not only with the attributes, thoughts, affinities, and contradictions that the author has written in, but also with a considerable unintended psychological presence. Drawing as he did on the circumstances of his own life—his tormented relationship with Frieda, or his love for his mother—Lawrence could hardly have been in control of all his attributions in his novels and stories. "Stuff" from the unconscious sticks all over intense works of the imagination.

While this in itself is not enough to guarantee animated life, the projections coming from the invested reader may provide the necessary spark. Under the right circumstances, whatever quasi-virtual status we confer on the activated character, this character's impact on the reader can be as great as that of certain "real" people in his life.

Rupert Birkin is my case in point. Even though more than thirty years have passed since my original reading of the book, his imprint on me remains perfectly distinct, as distinct as that left by any number of people from that time in my life—more distinct than some. "Knowing" him has, in that odd way of literature, mattered as much or more than knowing many people.

From the very first moment at the Crich wedding, when he appeared in the company of old Mr. Crich, the groom's father, and was described as thin, and then "pale and ill-looking," Birkin captured my attention. Maybe it was Lawrence's characterization, "[A]lthough he was dressed correctly for his part, yet there was an innate incongruity which caused a slight ridiculousness in his appearance." Or: "His nature was clever and separate, he did not fit at all in the conventional occasion." I'm not sure what snagged me at first contact. Very likely I connected with his outsiderness, the marginality that was more inborn than the product of some effort at "standing apart." I'm sure I liked the "clever and separate" because that was just how I felt at Cranbrook. Interestingly, the blond Nordic typology of Gerald Crich—objectively a sort of kinship—held no interest for me. It was his counterpart, his opposite, who compelled my best attention.

Birkin's magnetism was powerful. Although he was, in the obvious sense, a figment, I felt he exceeded me. He was smarter, subtler, and not at all predictable in the ways that counted. I couldn't see around him the way I feel I can see around most other characters; maybe for this reason I was blind to his "characterness." I felt that his relation to the world, as Lawrence set it out, was something I could aspire to. Not only could I annex him with my imagination, but I could invoke him to myself as a figure of counsel—*What would Birkin do?*—a reflex that powerfully amplified his reality status. I went around for many months carrying on, if not a dialogue, then a sustained monologue of which he was the main auditor. What's more, I loved that fact that our last names began with the same four letters—I was sure it was a sign of our secret kinship.

I accept the eroding work of time. From that first reading of the novel, as I said, I remember mainly those few postcard moments, and they are the more obvious scenic ones—Birkin rushing out into the fields and stripping off his clothes after the grim aesthete Hermione hits him with a paperweight; Birkin wrestling with Gerald; Birkin throwing stones at the pond in the moonlight when Ursula comes to find him. Behind these, more energy field than memory, is my sense of the man's aura, his unique presence, and here, as in life, once I have gotten to "know" someone in this way, there is no forgetting.

Of course I did the reader's work: I fired his character to life from the clues available, putting onto him a specificity that was not necessarily intended by the author. I don't know if Lawrence had in his mind a being quite as rounded or as consistently animated as the one I found, and this brings us right up against the mystery of how a writer possesses the characters he creates. Does he hold them in mind as bounded, freestanding entities, or does he proceed much more unconsciously, filling out a basic outline with gusts of expressive inspiration? Is his version of character continuous and sustained in his mind, or intermittent, subject to the ebbs and flows of his energy? I mean: did Lawrence have in mind *anything* like the independently motivated Rupert Birkin I encountered in these pages, or was that character, that particular bundle of energies, just a handy occasion for him to conduct his argument with existence?

My guess is that Birkin was for Lawrence a stand-in, a proxy figure into whom he freely poured his thoughts, emotions, confusions, and longings and that because of this he did not—could not—see him in the round. No more than any of us can see ourselves in the round. But if this is true then that vibrant spirit I felt I had internalized was more overtly than in most cases that of the author himself.

No matter how I try to explain the primary nature of the transaction, the fact is that I went around for quite some time under the powerful spell of a literary creation and my involvement changed my thinking; it introduced a presence through whom I could question and address the various circumstances of my life. Where before I had just chafed at the restrictions imposed by my parents, for instance, or the rules and expectations I found at school, now I could summon up the outspoken and independent-minded Birkin as my goad. I could picture him vividly and give inner voice to his contempt—his insistence on the needs of the unfettered spirit. This connection sometimes meant the difference between holding back at a certain moment and acting, or making my thoughts known plainly. I was far more likely to throw out an opinion post-Birkin, to self-consciously lay down my fork at the dinner table and say: "I don't buy that."

By way of Birkin, the active idea of him, I could not only see more clearly what I then knew to be the repressive machinery of the system, the social order, but I could think of my growing resistance as something noble, underwritten by a more daring interpretation of what life is and allows. Birkin boldly modeled for me the idea that a person should struggle to be a free spirit in the face of conformity, indeed that here was the essential human task.

Birkin's was not the one lone voice, of course. This was the decade of the 1960s and the idea of such struggle was gaining serious generational currency. There were writers, artists, musicians, and people in the movement—all testing and pushing, speaking out. They had come up around us like mushrooms in the night. Suddenly I could draw impulsive strength from many directions. But of the many voices out there, Birkin's (that is to say, Lawrence's) remained one of the most articulate, insistent, and persuasive. He was so free and lyrical in his expression, and he bowed to no social inhibition in confessing his disagreement.

Lawrence was hardly a minority taste back then. I don't exaggerate when I say that he had a stature and authority comparable to that of Virginia Woolf these days. He was viewed by many not just as a writer, but as an exemplar, a standard-bearer in what we knew was a collective battle against repression, hypocrisy, and cultural sclerosis. Earthy and free-spoken, a believer in instinct and emancipation and blood-knowledge (the taint of "fascism" was not yet on him), he refused to deny the force of sexual drives or the irrepressible unconscious energies. For a time he was everywhere, an early beneficiary of the paperback revolution, routinely assigned on college syllabi, conspicuous on coffee tables, along with R. D. Laing, Norman Mailer, Doris Lessing, Kurt Vonnegut, J. D. Salinger, and C. G. Jung. The eclipse in influence of this whole group in the last decades tells us as much about the patterns of social change as any transformations in fashion or music.

One marker of Lawrence's popularity, and a phenomenon greatly affecting my long-term relation to the novel, was the 1970 release of Ken

Russell's film of *Women in Love,* starring Alan Bates as Rupert Birkin, Oliver Reed as Gerald Crich, Glenda Jackson as Gudrun Brangwen, and Jennie Linden as her sister Ursula. As erratic and operatic, and errantly erotic, as Russell became in later films, here he showed a remarkable affinity for Lawrence's special ardor. Out of a novel that is significantly talk—voice thrown up against voice—he culled a sensuously emblematic narrative that not only preserved the basic architecture of the book, but somehow represented its essential arguments without indulging too much of Lawrence's theorizing.

I had only recently finished reading the novel when the film came out and, as can sometimes happen, the cinematic memories have to some degree usurped the cloudier, if also subtler, figments I had conjured for myself. The distinct images of the actors got in front of my own less externalized visualizations. From then on when I thought of Birkin I pictured Alan Bates, and so on. Would this have happened with a less inspired cast or a less viscerally compelling movie? Probably not. I know that I can think of Malcolm Lowry's novel *Under the Volcano* without picturing Albert Finney as the Consul, never mind that Finney is a great actor and John Huston an estimable director. Nor have Jeremy Irons or James Mason displaced my nonspecific image of Humbert Humbert. But Alan Bates was not only close to how I featured Birkin (and, at one remove, Lawrence himself), but he was so attractive in the part that I *wanted* Birkin to look thus.

No less impressive and influential was Glenda Jackson in the part of Gudrun, the willful, wasp-tongued sister (who I later learned was modeled on the writer Katherine Mansfield). It was as if Jackson had put her interpretive signature once and for all on the elemental essence of Gudrun's character, which was sharp enough in the novel, but very nearly archetypal on the screen. I mean Gudrun's focus on sexual power, her relentless working of the lever of male self-esteem, her perfectly choreographed swings between invitation and refusal. Intrigued as I was by this when I was reading (it was all new information for me then), when I sat in the dark movie theater I found myself mesmerized by the gestural performance, the scornful way she tightened her lips, her dare-extending smile, and the ironic vigilance that could slip in a second from the playful to the menacing.

By now it should be clear that I am not so much interested in discussing *Women in Love* on its own merits as a novel so much as tracing some of the different threads of influence it has spun out—as part of the counter-cultural Zeitgeist, or, more personally, as an active agitating force in my thought-life. *Women in Love* fascinates me because my response to the book was from the first so bound up with the *idea* of Lawrence. Lawrence the emblem, the man who was the first to give me the idea—through his writing as well as through the intensity of my attributions—that living was above all a struggle to create, or maybe salvage, a soul. Indeed, the feeling of this was so strong that I believe I derived it even before reading the work for myself, drawing it down from the air around Vicky, Jim, and Mark, from the way they acted and spoke. It was so clearly what I wanted to hear about at that point in my life. I did not so much read him as pace this way and that inside his dense romantic landscape.

ALTHOUGH LAWRENCE, like any true inspiration, never disappeared from my life, his influence receded for a time, much as Salinger's had. I graduated from Cranbrook and grew away from Vicky and the others. When I got to college, I read angry and despairing writers by the armful—Henry Miller, Louis-Ferdinand Celine, Jean Genet—and joined my whole generation in its highly publicized search for authenticity. Lawrence was always there in the vicinity, but he didn't become a focus again until in the middle of my junior year I got involved with Jess, whom I'd known when we were in grade school together. This proved to be the core event—adventure—of my growing up, and when I look back from the vantage of three decades, I can see how Lawrence is woven through it all.

First there was the Gudrun/Glenda Jackson connection. For what drew me irresistibly to Jess, apart from our childhood bond and the appeal of her prettiness, was the very specific air of challenge she exuded. She was exceptionally well-read; she had a sardonic verbal agility I had never encountered. She had a way of taking me on, too, especially at the beginning, that was at once admiring and testing, as if each comment and comeback were being scored; as if my male fitness were being checked and re-evaluated at every moment. *You have been weighed in the balance and you have been found wanting.* It was as serious as it was playful, as daunting as it was stimulating. I had never had to rally myself with an-other person in this way before. I was completely hooked.

As early as our first date I made the connection. In her style of provo-cation, in her way of responding—barbed, insinuating, sublimely ironic—Jess reminded me of Jackson's Gudrun, only without quite the same edge of aggression. I told her as much and she was, as I remember, amused. Amused in her Gudrun way, managing with a laugh and a glance to sug-gest that this information, too, had some bearing on how she might judge my essential worth.

Part of the attraction of the Gudrun type is that so long as she confers benediction you feel that you are succeeding on a very high level, earn-ing an esteem that is reaffirmed at every moment. This was the feeling I had at first with Jess, before we knew each other well. Later that sense of incessant testing fell away, but I remember how early on that look of mockery incited me. One night, I remember, I suddenly stood up in the middle of a disagreement and flung a full bottle of red wine against the wall of my room, spattering everything in sight—I didn't feel she was tak-ing me seriously enough.

If anything consoled me during this hyperintense period of courtship, it was that even if Jess was, in certain ways, like Gudrun, I was nothing like Gerald, Gudrun's classic adversary, and Jess's mockery was not meant, as Gudrun's always seemed to be, to be sexually belittling.

I can't guess how I would understand that first big relationship—or any other—without benefit of all that I absorbed from my reading of Lawrence. At the same time—now that I've gone back and re-read *Women in Love*—I realize how thin and simplistic my reading must have been. I'm sure that I grasped that the Gerald/Gudrun struggle took place at the level of primal wills, but I really had no idea how deep—how absolute—the standoff was for Lawrence, how much it drew on the battleground events of his own marriage. I think I believed—and this, if anything, is a sign of youth—that these absolute disagreements might be resolved, that understanding would lead to correction and solution. I couldn't yet conceive that an erotic relationship could be a fight to the finish—the finish being not death (though for Gerald it was), but the ultimate capitulation of one partner to the other.

I don't mean it to sound like every relationship is, at root, a pitched battle—many aren't—only that insofar as the wills express themselves there seem to be no easily negotiated solutions. The will is an imperious force, not susceptible to reason or emotional adjustment. It is, like sexuality, blind and anarchic. Although it can to some extent be masked and controlled, held in check, these efforts do not affect its nature at all; it lives unheeding behind the Potemkin Village of our socialized behavior.

While our will can certainly express itself in sexual terms—it did between Gudrun and Gerald—its operations are in no way confined to erotic give-and-take. Far more common and persuasive are the combats of daily life that take the outward form of deal-making—the familiar resistance and acquiescence scenarios of domestic life—but that have as their real inward stakes the preservation of personal autonomy, indeed personality itself. Here I can only generalize, but as a longtime observer of relationships, marital and otherwise, I have yet to find a long-term couple not deeply marked by the abrasions of self against self. The successful relationships, it seems, have been those that have found how to make this friction into a style, a kind of performance mitigated from both sides by a certain humorous tolerance.

There is no humor in Lawrence. He is, as the saying goes, "as serious as a heart attack," and this might be one reason why his vision can seem so absolute, so dark. Colliding wills have little recourse in this scheme of things. I don't think I grasped this when I first read *Women in Love.* I may have even viewed Birkin and Ursula as a romantic success story. I don't think I got that Birkin's final reply to Ursula's assertion of the absolute sufficiency of the man/woman love bond—"I don't believe that"—was not a conversational retort, but a marking of the final distance, an admission of the fatally compromised nature of his and Ursula's marriage. His words have the weight of a "never again," and I now suspect that it was out of a fear that we might miss this that Ken Russell underlined that last moment of the film with a dramatic musical swipe.

Reflecting on Lawrence in this open, omnidirectional way, I see how easily any assertion can become its own new track. Forward progress depends on resisting possibilities. For instance, I want to think about why this writer was so right, so important for the early years of the counter-culture, how his restless combative vision inflamed so many of us. It was not just that he pitched against rigid morality and the tyrannies of owner-ship and exclusivity, though that was a big part of the appeal. He was also a man unafraid of the idea of spirit, and his fiction presented a single living world: things flamed and flared and pulsed. If relationships were struggles, red in tooth and claw, they were also alive with the promise of merging—and this was very much the ethos of communal hippie America in the late 1960s and early '70s.

Likewise, there are long passages to be written on the waning of that influence. The Lawrence fascination did not outlive the counterculture, really. Rock & roll endured the great reaction of the mid-1970s, but the author of *Lady Chatterley's Lover* and *The Rainbow* did not fare as well. His blood-cult tendencies, caricatures of the original romantic sensual-ism, finished him off—those, and the bourgeoning Women's Movement, which was not about to countenance so stark a depiction of psycho-erotic combat between the sexes.

But for all of the possible topics—I haven't even mentioned the more literary examination of narrative or style—I found myself drawn in most this time by the personal, by the reactions that became immediate in my thinking when I re-read the novel. Love, will, exclusivity—I have consid-ered these. What I have not yet touched on is the extent to which these are entwined with the theme of the eroticism of friendship.

This is what underlies Birkin's denial of Ursula. He cannot imagine a full existence that does not balance against heterosexual love some counter-part love for a man—the kind of compelling physical and emotional pull that he felt for Gerald, a pull charged but not homoerotic. What a liber-ating, frightening conception—that one could admit the love of a friend and do so without crossing the sexual boundary. Much was made of this, I remember, by Vicky, Mark, and Jim. And later by me. Reading Lawrence at seventeen, filtering the surges of my emotional life through the figure of

Birkin, I know I felt easier in my few deep male friendships—I didn't have to see my intense feelings as a threat to my sexual self-identity. I needed Lawrence for that part of my coming-of-age.

The Birkin question remains, though, how much married love excludes, or takes the place of other, parallel loves. I don't know that now, decades later, I'm any closer to the answer. That final passage still gives me a deep pang. Like Birkin, I still wonder if our culture, for all its vaunted permissiveness, isn't still walled in by its rigid definitions. We may be more tolerant of overtly gay relationships in some ways than of friendships that transcend our categories of comfort. Again, Lawrence triggers this questioning, but he takes us no further than Birkin's pained perplexity.

We all know that there is no returning—ever—to the book one remembers, and that our visits are, assuming that we still remember the first encounter, one of the surest ways we have of judging how we have changed over time. Most books, not surprisingly, reveal their slightness, refusing to hold our new projections; they make us wonder what it was that had captivated us. Only a few work the other way, revealing all of the nuances that we read right past and—it can happen—flinging our former naïveté into our faces.

Re-reading *Women in Love,* my main response was amazement at my own callow youthfulness. I had somehow stored the novel in memory as a sweepingly romantic work of literature. From the charged evocations of nature, certainly. Lawrence was a celebrant of landscape, and the novel, like all his work, is rich with the Keatsian "poetry of Earth." And possibly from some of the early scenes that establish Birkin as the archetypal impassioned searcher. But working through the book now that I'm older—married, a father, much more wised-up to how it really is between men and women—I was struck by the man's deep pessimism. *Everything* this time seemed to boil down to the grappling of wills, the primal struggle for ascendancy. I could feel myself beginning to resist. If this is an aspect of human relations that is too often covered over or ignored, it's still not the whole story. The author's vision of dueling wills looks right past the grand noun of the title—love—or at least radically reduces its field of influence.

Love, for Lawrence, is not finally the liberation we yearn for, but is rather a sacrifice of our core autonomy to a force that would bind and hold. We see this so clearly at novel's end. Again, I look to that last scene. Birkin has been grieving beside the body of his dead friend Gerald, the man he felt was his blood-brother. Ursula, upset by the intensity of his reaction, asks (as she has several times before): "Aren't I enough for you?" To which Birkin, ever truthful, replies, "No."

My more recent—my grown-up—reading has me divided against myself. On the one hand, I find myself chafing against Lawrence's insistence on the near-absolute dominance of will. On the other, seeing that dynamic anatomized, I have to grant how frighteningly insightful he was about how as lovers we battle for possession. He asked as few writers have: what is love, what are its parts, and how does it work?

I found myself pulled most awake—made to feel that important things in my life were at stake—by the short chapter (XIII) called "Mino." Coming in the earlier part of the novel, "Mino" centers on a dialogue about love between Birkin and Ursula. Here Birkin expresses most fully his romantic and spiritual ideal and maps out the one understanding of love that stands free of the entanglement of possessive wills. His is a singular and elusive notion, so elusive that Ursula—for whom love between a man and a woman is all-embracing, all-consuming, admitting no third party—can't grasp it at all.

What Birkin proposes is a love based not on emotion but on spiritual recognition, one that seeks to honor the integrity of the other rather than annex it. It is a love of the Rilkean "love me, love my solitude" sort. At the same time it is an absolute. As Birkin explains to Ursula: ". . . if we are going to know each other, we must pledge ourselves for ever. If we are going to make a relationship, even of friendship, there must be something final and infallible about it." He goes on: "At any rate, I don't feel the emotion of love for you—no, and I don't want to. Because it gives out in the last issues." And: "There is a real impersonal me, that is beyond love, beyond any emotional relationship." And still later, "What I want is a strange conjunction with you . . . not meeting and mingling . . . but an equilibrium, a pure balance of two single beings. . . ."

Is this possible—a love that finds its highest consummation outside the charged arena of the emotions? Can we speak of a love that is not itself an emotion, that is not subject to the almost subatomic yearning of one for another, and that is therefore not linked to the erotic will? I would never have thought so. I haven't met with such a thing myself, at least never in the romantic sphere, but I caught myself heeding Birkin's words closely. I tuned into a vision that presented something more like what I have found in friendships, where I have known deep affection with little or no pressure toward exclusivity; where feelings have grown naturally from shared experience and recognized personal affinities. Although these relationships can be strongly emotional, they are without a will toward a merging of identities; it is possible to experience emotions for themselves and not as part of a "tending toward."

I had to wonder why Birkin needed to ask for a pledge, an implicit commitment to ongoingness, to the poet's "for ever." It seemed at first an admission of uncertainty, a lack of trust. Once I might have said it was. Now it seems clear enough: affirming an absolute devotion is here not, as it is in marriage, a binding action, a quasi-contractual gesture; for Birkin it's the reverse. The affirmation is what locates the bond outside of time, removing it from contingency, and offers a platform of freedom. Rather than marking an apotheosis of emotional investment, it looks to place the relationship beyond the mutuality of the affections. It anchors love not in feeling, but in the certainty of a soul-bond that will be impervious to all cycling of feeling; it is a gesture *à deux,* a self-transcendence.

I can't express this more precisely. I only know that when I engaged Birkin's peculiar passion this time around, it rang out more clearly than anything in the novel. With his view in mind I was able to find contour for what has been inchoate in my thinking for some time. A wish—a faith— was clarified for me, if not an explanation that would support it.

What I find remarkable now is that Lawrence has given this vision of love beyond possession to a relatively young man, for it seems to me very much a view (and longing) that one comes to later in life. I'm startled, too, to find that Birkin's philosophy represents a concerted effort to escape from the tentacles of possessive love, rather than a preemptive move. In other words, one would have needed a long schooling in Ursuline exclusivity before building up sufficient escape velocity. Here I can only guess at how it was for Lawrence and Frieda, and whether he used Birkin, so similar to himself in certain of his particulars, not least appearance, as a mouthpiece for his own deepest desires.

I'VE BEEN LOOKING for a way to circle back around to the question of how we view the books of our youth as we age away from them. Serendipity just answered, reminding me of something I have wondered about often. In the note about Lawrence at the front of my paperback copy of *Women in Love,* I read: "In 1930 he died in Vence, in the south of France, at the age of forty-four." If I looked at those dates when I first read the novel, when I was seventeen, I likely did not reflect on them as I do now, in my midfifties. Forty-four then was a marker in the indeterminate future; it meant "all the time in the world." It did not mean: this man who burned his brand onto our literature, who wrote so many stories, poems, essays, travelogues, who wrote *Sons and Lovers, The Rainbow,* and *Lady Chatterley's Lover,* died when he was nearly eight years younger than I am now. Truly, if anything can change one's understanding and appreciation of a work of art, it's this realization. The novel I had read *toward* as a young man, mining it for the deep wisdoms of a grown man, I now read, at least at some level, *away from,* seeing its truths, but also tagging those truths as belonging to a younger man—Lawrence was twenty-eight when he wrote *Women in Love.* At this point I want to underscore the fact of the achievement, which Lawrence could only have attained with the pressure and decisiveness that come when a writer truly believes he has seen into the way of things and needs to deliver the news. If only for this reason, his young age bears no real relation to the perspectives we've adopted in our strange youth-minded culture.

Romancing the Self

Gustave Flaubert's *Madame Bovary*

I FIRST READ *Madame Bovary* in July of 1971 in a bunkhouse in Deer Lodge, Montana. I was nineteen years old and had gotten myself a summer job that gratified all of my fantasies about meeting the "authentic" face to face. I'd been hired as an all-purpose "hand" on the Tavener Ranch, at that time the largest cattle operation in the western part of the state. I spent my days bucking bales of hay onto a long wagon and then riding from place to place behind an old John Deere as my partner, Tom Bolton, drove. I'd jump up at each stop to break up a dozen bales with a small hatchet and push the hay out to the cattle that started massing together as soon as they heard the approaching sputter of our engine. The days were long and full of honorable hard work; the setting was ruggedly beautiful, and there were actual craggy, hard-bitten cowboys everywhere, silhouetted on horseback on the ridges, driving their pickup trucks with dusty abandon along the access roads—there were even a few in the bunkhouse where I stayed.

Not that any of them had more than a bemused, weary nod to offer a college boy with long curly hair. They walked around me with that bone-weary bowlegged gait I so admired, and they talked right past me. Indeed, their life at the ranch went on so successfully without the slightest reference to me that I soon gave up my fantasies of poker and beer with the boys and took up my real summer residence in the familiar solitude of books. Whenever I got a minute, I threw myself down on my bed and read. I was, however—and this I quickly discovered—understocked. There were no bookstores or libraries within an hour's driving range, and I had only the few paperbacks I had brought along. My small library included, I remember, Jack Kerouac's *Desolation Angels* (part of my counterculture syllabus), a few novels of the sort I read in those days—one by John Barth, another by J. P. Donleavy—and then there was *Madame Bovary,* a book I had brought along as a kind of default option after one of my routine self-improvement resolutions.

Madame Bovary was, I knew, a certified classic, part of the great Western canon, though to be honest, I don't think I knew what a canon was back then, never mind that I was a declared English major at the University of Michigan. This was, remember, the dawn of the 1970s, and for those of us living the ethos of the times, believing in the imminent transformation of society, there was nothing as suspicious as a work certified by the culture of reactionary elders.

What was the book doing in my backpack? If I can reconstruct my reasoning, there was a kind of reversing strategy at work. I didn't nec-essarily want to read the novel, but I wanted it—along with various other authorized classics—under my belt so that I could put a finer edge on my "brilliant-sloucher" routine, the triumph of which would come when some exasperated professor hailed me in my back-row seat and fed me a challenging question I could answer by saying, "Well, Flaubert got there first, I believe—" The embarrassing thing I need to admit is that I didn't yet know to silence the "t" in the author's last name. Had my moment come I would have tripped headlong over my own arrogance.

In any event, I was in Montana, ignored and lonely, and I had within a few weeks gone through my whole stock of "reads"—all except *Madame Bovary.* There was nothing for me to do but take it up—"it," the dread classic, the very title of which I found off-putting: the heroine's last name sounded like an unfortunate conflation of "bovine" and "ovary" and seemed to hint at something rurally gynecological (not inappropriate, given my setting and duties). But faced as I was with inner desolation, I read and read, and what sharp surprise I felt there, hunched up on my prison-issue bed alongside the jokey "Gone Fishin'" calendar on which every night I inked a bold X into the day's square. Quite simply, I fell in. I transported myself in mind with astonishing ease to provincial France in the early decades of the 1800s, and lost all proper sense of awe before the classic as I felt—as millions had before me—the bitter clench of fate on the extravagantly foolish life of Emma Bovary.

What I remember from that first reading is the marveling sense of displacement I felt as I looked up from, say, the scene of Emma attending her first opera, to stare, almost uncomprehendingly, at the unfinished 2 x 4 studs marking the passage from one barren bunkhouse room to another. But I know that there was also a new sense of opening vistas that came with the realization, new for me, that something certified as classic could also be the source of the highest pleasure. Did I vow then—I can almost imagine I did—that I would from then on dedicate myself to the reading of great works of literature? I can't swear to that. But I do know that after this first encounter I had much less hesitation about picking up these forbidding items. A few that gratified me in the following year were, I recall, Thomas Mann's *Buddenbrooks*, Stendhal's *The Red and the Black*, and some of the easy early novels of Henry James.

Taking the essayist's license, I leave the young man in that bunkhouse in his favorite position, under covers, head propped high by available pillows, bedside lamp stripped of its cheap shade in the interest of maximal illumination, and jump a good distance forward in time. The self-styled restless wanderer, now in his late thirties, has settled down. I am living in Cambridge, Massachusetts, working in a bookstore, as I have been for years, reading with what has always felt like a late-comer's zeal. After long struggle I have given up on my ambition to write a novel. I have, instead, begun to write nonfiction—essays, reviews, criticism—for any place that will publish my words, and I am just breaking my way into teaching. Harvard Summer School is an early venue. There I preside over a self-designed class in which I lead a small group (mostly adults) through the paces of applied criticism. We read and discuss a handful of novels, and then I set out various critical tasks for them. One of the books on the syllabus—because I know it is inexhaustibly teachable, and because I still remember my first entranced reading—is *Madame Bovary*. In our well-lit room up in Lamont Library, armed with a kit bag of literary theories I've been studying, I work to guide my group into the brave new world of interpretation.

The whole process feels heady, intellectually prosperous. We are now in the 1980s—historical context is everything in these matters—in the glory days of theory in academia. There is a great deal of available energy in the air. Those of us with any literary pretensions are all hyped up—pro and con—by the procedures of structuralism, deconstruction, reader-response theory, you name it. Flaubert's novel falls to our blades like a fine cut of meat as we fillet, carve, slice, and dice up the text. We read the scenes for their "tropes" and "subtexts," unpack the symbolic logic of images, search out parallel structures, ponder tensions, and truffle for buried ideologies; we disinter gender biases and apply informed psychoanalytic templates; we examine politics of race and class. We cycle through a dozen different interpretive modalities, overlooking nothing, except—it now occurs to me—the life of the novel itself. But those were the times.

Thinking back on this era, not just my teaching life, but my writing life as well, I see now how much I was under the sway of another powerful mythology. If in my original reading I'd had to face and overcome the tyranny of the classic—that idealized view of the sovereign seriousness of high culture—then during this period I was very much in the grip of a different tyranny, the idea of Flaubert as the god of the sentence. Like many would-be writers, I had been greatly influenced by stories of Flaubert's grail-quest for *le mot juste,* the exact word, which of course translated into the ideal of the perfect sentence, paragraph, chapter . . . book. The author's legendary daylong struggles with the wording of single sentences, his well-known funks, his *marinades,* testified to his belief that there was an ultimate, attainable prose; that the hard-won calibration of sounds, rhythms, textures, and echoes could find imperishable sequences for words, a notion as profound as any philosophy. It was, in fact, a philosophy, one which granted to language the potential to verbally incarnate the reality it served.

The idea was enough to make the head spin around. In my case, I know, it led to long hours at the desk, hours in which success was measured less by fluency of output than by the intensity of my combat with the means of expression. I was haunted by the fantasy of "getting it right," whatever "it" was—of expressing myself with such accurate inevitability that the words I typed would feel as if they were chiseled into the white of the page.

For years and years, until it yellowed and curled, I kept a quotation from a letter Flaubert had written to George Sand tacked to the wall by my writing desk, positioned so I would have to see it whenever I looked up. It was the most distilled possible expression of the faith—the mysticism— that underlies the doctrine of *le mot juste:*

> When I come upon a bad assonance or repetition in my sentences, I'm sure I'm floundering in the false. By searching I find the proper expression, which is always the only one, and which is also harmonious. The word is never lacking when one possesses the idea. Is there not, in this precise fitting of parts, something eternal, like a principle? If not, why should there be a relation between the right word and the musical word? Or why should the greatest compression of thought always result in a line of poetry?

The implications of Flaubert's assertion are extraordinary—the verbal expression and the essential nature of the thing expressed might be in some fundamental alignment, a kind of enduring exactitude is possible. Imagine how a possibility like this might torment an idealistic young writer. It tormented me for years. Indeed, so long as I aspired to write fiction, which I did until I was nearly thirty, the wavering mirage of perfect incarnated language insured that almost nothing I wrote would escape the wastebasket. I spent years knotted up with the feeling of my artistic inadequacy. Nothing I wrote survived the test. Every word seemed provisional, hesitantly affixed to the page, liable to correction, erasure, or replacement. What an extraordinary relief I felt, at some level, when I gave up the quest for the perfect fiction and turned instead to nonfiction—the review, the essay—where this particular tyranny did not feel so absolute.

But so far as teaching went, Flaubert's struggle to wrestle his *Bovary* into being put the bar up as high as it could go. It also authorized us as

readers to push at the text with full interrogating pressure. With a work so
perfect, so *realized*, so beyond accident, every suspicion was true—every
pattern, convergence, suggestion, and implication. Flaubert, a god, had
seen it all; whatever any of us found was most certainly part of the intended totality. This was exalting. You could push and push and be sure
that the structure was not going to collapse on you.

What were some of the things we discussed and wrote about? There
was, to take an instance, the matter of Charles Bovary's famous hat, that
ridiculous elaborate artifact so laboriously described in the opening section. "It was a headgear of composite order," wrote Flaubert, "containing
elements of an ordinary hat, a hussar's busby, a lancer's cap, a sealskin
cap and a nightcap: one of those wretched things whose mute hideous-
ness suggests unplumbed depths, like an idiot's face." And he goes on
for several long sentences naming its ill-sorted parts. We all wondered,
of course, why an artist so much in command of the least detail should
have lavished such care on the peculiar construction of such a seemingly
inconsequential item. It took Vladimir Nabokov, in his published lecture
on the novel, to enlighten us: the hat was at once itself, a hat, and a cunningly composed cipher, a deliberate system of layers meant to alert the
watchful reader to the fact that the whole novel was a strategically devised
artifact; this was one of its many inwoven secrets. As Nabokov writes: "the
image is developed layer by layer, tier by tier, room by room, coffin by coffin," whereupon he connects it to Charles and Emma's wedding cake, the
layout of their house, on and on, all the way along to Charles's peculiar
request for his dear wife's burial—that there be three coffins, one nested
inside the other like those Russian dolls. Nabokov, the subtlest of crafts-
men himself, pounced on the detail; Flaubert could only have dreamed of
such a reader.

Certainly we talked in class about the prose itself, the material density
that was one of the fruits of the author's incessant hunt for *le mot juste*.
Precision, the fanatical attention to detail, the evoking power of images
and carefully assembled sequences of images—of course we considered all
of these things. But we pushed further, gave ourselves over several times
to orgies of magnified close reading. Hovering over a passage, tracking it

phrase by phrase, we theorized about how Flaubert's particular juxtaposition of details played on the reader's senses in a carefully worked-out sequence. We may well have studied this description from the ball at La Vaubyessard:

> Here the air was warm and fragrant; the scent of flowers and fine linen mingled with the odor of cooked meats and truffles. Candle flames cast long gleams on rounded silver dish-covers; the clouded facets of the cut glass shone palely; there was a row of bouquets all down the table; and on the wide-bordered plates the napkins stood like bishops' mitres, each with an oval-shaped roll between its folds. Red lobster claws protruded from platters; oversized fruit was piled up on moss in openwork baskets; quail were served in their plumage; steam rose from open dishes; and the platters of carved meat were brought around by the maître d'hotel himself, grave as a judge in silk stockings, knee breeches, white neckcloth and jabot. He reached them down between the guests, and with a flick of his spoon transferred to each plate the piece desired. Atop the high copper-banded porcelain stove the statue of a woman swathed to the chin in drapery stared down motionless at the company.

So smooth is the writing, so inviting the details, that the reader may be tempted to believe that they fell naturally into place, which of course they did not. Flaubert took hitherto unheard of pains to move his reader first here, then here, then here, appealing to one sense, then another, making sure that the eye stayed busy, formulating the gleaming candlelight "on rounded silver dish-covers" and the protruding red claws, and rising steam, all of the elements held together, figuratively anyway, by the staring statue on top of the stove.

The effect of these shifts of scale and focus, coming as they do very rapidly in confined quarters, is to heighten the sense of illusionistic dimension. The operation in the mind's eye is maybe not so different from the exertion by which we turn jumbled geometric shapes into suddenly volume-rich panoramas when we look at Cubist paintings. This is one of Flaubert's great and subtle triumphs: he can pack his descriptive scenes with sensory elements in such a way that they expand, and then keep expanding in retrospect, growing behind us while we are not looking, so that a brief passage, like the one from the ball, blossoms in the memory like one of those cunningly folded Japanese flowers that you place in a bowl of water. The subtle phenomenon helps to explain while reading the novel, we experience an ever-intensifying sense of being in a complex tactile world governed by gravity and laws of perspective, very nearly containing its own autonomous weather systems.

WRITERS, even would-be writers, reading *Madame Bovary* cannot avoid having their attention drawn repeatedly to the procession of perfectly managed effects. Flaubert is so thrilling in his way of matching craft to content— like the comic alternation at the agricultural fair of Emma and Rodolphe's escalating intimacy with the flashed reports from the awards presentation— that the reader often finds his attention divided as by a presentation on a split screen, heeding the how almost as much as the what. Amazingly, the one focus does not seem to undermine the other. Awareness of the technical mastery might distract on one level, but the brilliance also has a way of trumping that critical recognition and pulling us ever deeper into the work. I can grant that there is high-level craft bringing me the elongation of the candle flames on the rounded dish-covers, but even as I admire I am drawn more fully into seeing. When we are compelled, as here, to bring an augmented attention to bear, we stretch inwardly to overcome the contradiction.

Or maybe—if this is a book we return to over and over—we experience its different levels in alternation, remarking the prodigious craft one time so that we can better take it on trust the next.

This second theory might be one way for me to account for what I feel is the next stage in my decades-long effort to take the measure of *Madame Bovary*. This, combined with the never-to-be-discounted factor of simply growing older and getting more experience of the world. Recently, after such a long time during which I was preoccupied with the complexity of the novel, and the analysis of that complexity, I am again able to read it for what it essentially is—a tragic story, a dramatization of the old adage that "character is destiny." Reading the book now, as a man in my early fifties, I am closer to the spirit of my original encounter than I have been for decades. I don't know if this level of immediacy would have been possible without those years of formal interpretation and pattern-seeking.

I was profoundly moved by the novel all through my most recent rereading. I felt distinctly that my increased life-experience—having suffered jealousy, remorse, the loss of love, and lived the daily discipline of marriage and fatherhood—allowed me to move past my long-held view of Emma, exchanging a somewhat simple view for a far more conflicted and interesting one.

According to my original understanding, Emma was a vain, weak-willed, romantically impressionable woman whose appetites had been fanned to a blaze by her exposure to sentimental romances, and who ended up paying with her life for her refusal of the reality principle, the principle presented in such amusing caricature by the counterpoint figure of the pharmacist Homais, who swims around in the common world like an oblivious fish.

I don't mean to say that I stopped seeing this as Emma's character—I didn't—but now instead of resting in judgment, instead of concentrating my main response on the terror and pity that mark our encounters with the tragic, I also registered a tender protectiveness that felt like something new. The more we experience, I think, the more our tolerance for human weakness increases. I remarked not only the foolishness, the obviously mediocre content of much of Emma's inner life, but I also found myself tuning into what that ceaseless daydreaming represented. For as common as her grandiose fancies may be at times, they do stand—much as do Don Quixote's—for the aspiring part of our nature. They are, even in their selfishness and simplicity, nobler than the universal pull toward accommodation, which in Flaubert's portrayal of bourgeois reality is like the force of gravity.

In my reader's heart, I often side with Emma Bovary—certainly in the opening sections of the novel—even as I am shaking my head at her astonishing naïveté, her cupidity, her sexual greed. I side with her—or, better, am *made* to side with her—much in the same way that I am brought around to sympathy for the monstrous Humbert Humbert in *Lolita*. And with the same effect: I experience a complicated self-division. Could it be that this split-reader dynamic is partly responsible for my sense of intensified *investment* in the novel? Reading *Madame Bovary* I am much more *there* than I am with so many other works that I read. Tensions and contradictions *do* increase the voltage, even as they decimate my usual placidity, my complacencies. My contemplation of Emma gets me going.

THIS WRESTLING, this disputatious inner swing defines engaged reading. A great writer in creating a world takes hold of reality and human character so fully that we are denied equilibrium; we can never rest in full satisfaction the way we can with lesser writers who sell us the comfort of resolution. A great character is one who perpetually eludes the contours we draw for that character. Think of Raskolnikov, Isabel Archer, even Ahab. To know all may, indeed, be to pardon all, but to know all is also to live with the disconcerting vibration of contradictions and conflicting responses. Certainly this is true with Emma Bovary, whose immensity as a figure in my imagination is the immensity of a single soul seen through to its complex depths. Never mind that in many ways she is as shallow as can be—insofar as she is a romantic dreamer, she exceeds my grasp. Desire is always greater than the explanations we offer for it.

Emma Bovary, the pretty, nervous, birdlike woman struggling inside the confines of her marriage in a provincial French town in the 1830s, has me compelled and intrigued and set up against myself. The whole long process begins with a glimpse of a "young woman wearing a blue merino dress with three flounces," who comes to her father's farmhouse door to greet the young doctor, and continues through all kinds of situations and crises, right up to Emma's horrifying death struggle, which has to rival that of Tolstoy's Ivan Ilich, and which by his own report made Flaubert quite literally ill during the writing of the scene. We see Emma from every side. Even so, there are moments when I suddenly think I get who and what she really is. I had a striking instance of this in my last reading, a classic illustration of a Freudian "slip." About a third of the way through the book, before Emma had even had her first affair—with Leon—I read, or thought I read, the following: "Charles was in a gloomy state: he had no patients. He sat silent for hours on end, took naps in his consulting room, or watched his wife as she screwed." Well, of course that last word is "sewed." And I pounced on the slip and corrected it. But even as I did I caught myself thinking, with a righteous decisiveness, *But yes, this* is *the whole novel in fact. Charles stands by while she screws.* And at one level this is the succinct reduced truth of things. But it took the slip, the misreading, for me to see it and to feel in myself the flash of judgment. *Emma had sexual liaisons behind Charles's back—she's nothing but a little slut and she deserves what she gets.* The reaction came leaping out in front of any subtler, more reasoned character analysis. I had to grant that it was one of the truths of my experience of the novel.

But only *one* of the truths. If it were the only one the novel would have long ago gone dead on me; it would be little more than an artistically drawn cautionary tale. It is cautionary, of course, but not at this simplistic and moralistic level. No, the ways in which *Madame Bovary* extends its warnings have little to do with paying the price for adulterous transgression and everything to do with paying the toll on an ungoverned narcissistic grandiosity. This was the big realization of my most recent reading, which cut to the very core of the novel for me and accounted for much of its harrowing power.

Madame Bovary is, I see now, not just a novel about an adulteress who recklessly mortgages her husband's finances until he is ruined, and who then, faced with exposure, takes her life. It is, beyond that, a dramatic re-creation of the stages by which an idle dissatisfaction, stoked by fantasies— many of them inspired by her reading—becomes a deluded, compulsive quest for rescue, for an unattainable romantic apotheosis, which often feels like a misdirected quest for the absolute. This was no doubt rooted in her emotionally charged early religious upbringing in which, as is not uncommon, Christ himself was represented almost as a figure in a romance. At some point Emma's quest becomes something more than just a bored woman's distraction; at some point she gives over her volition, her control—much as a nun might for her faith—and this makes her destruction inevitable. She moves from being an agent in her life to being a pawn of circumstance.

The frightening thing here, so similar to what Leo Tolstoy does with the story of Anna Karenina, is Flaubert's depiction of the gradual loss of center, the sacrifice of common sense and a relational connection to others to dreams, dreams that change by degrees from harmless pleasure to hopeless addiction and create a cycle in which every disappointment, every failed rescue, leads Emma to up the ante, fantasizing, necessarily, a greater compensating consummation, much as the losing gambler needs to put larger stakes on each turn of the wheel in hopes of recouping his losses. Flaubert's message would seem to be that dreams ultimately undermine the character because they make dailiness ever harder to bear and drive the dreamer further and further from reality, not just the reality of immediate surroundings, but the reality of other people. Over the course of the novel, scene by scene, Emma becomes ever more the grandiose narcissist, though she imagines it is love that drives her. No person matters, not Charles, not her little daughter—only the idea of her lover, be it Leon or Rodolphe. She heeds nothing except what relates to her mania. Everything else is thrown on the pyre.

The situation might be different if genuine love were the cause—powerful feeling for another person whom she saw and knew in the I-Thou way, where the Other is confronted and engaged. But Emma's lovers, Leon and Rodolphe, are finally pretext figures. They are essential not in and of themselves—she hardly reckons them as individuals—but as agents of the fantasy. They serve the perpetuation of the script—the self-script—in her mind.

What a radical thing Flaubert has done in this little book. He has stripped the pretty covering, the poetic sanction, away from romantic love, that vaporous loss of boundaries, that aggrandized melting away of self, to show it for what it so often is: a deeply egotistical flight from the real. Here is how he describes at one point Emma's approach to Rouen, where she went weekly to meet Leon:

> A kind of intoxication was wafted up to her from those closely
> packed lives, and her heart swelled as though the 120,000 souls
> palpitating below had sent up to her as a collective offering the

breath of all the passions she supposed them to be feeling. In the face of the vastness her love grew larger, and was filled with a turmoil that echoed the vague ascending hum. All this love she, in turn, poured out—onto the squares, onto the tree-lined avenues, onto the streets; and to her the old Norman city was like some fabulous capital, a Babylon into which she was making her entry.

This is the world seen as stage set, an unreal inflation of self's desire masking itself as an oceanic embrace of reality. But the key word in the passage is "Babylon," a figure for all that is prideful and corrupt.

Two pages later, Flaubert shows us Emma and Leon together in their love nest:

They lunched beside the fire, on a little table inlaid with rose-wood. Emma carved, murmuring all kinds of endearments as she put the pieces on his plate; and she gave a loud, wanton laugh when the champagne foamed over the fine edge of the glass onto the rings on her fingers. They were so completely lost in their possession of each other that they thought of themselves as being in their own home, destined to live there for the rest of their days, eternal young husband and eternal young wife.

How frightening and sobering it is for Emma directly after her tryst to encounter the grotesque beggar. He is walking along the roadside as she is making her way back to Yonville in the coach. "His clothes were a mass of rags," writes Flaubert, "and his face was hidden under a battered old felt hat that was turned down all around like a basin; when he took this off, it was to reveal two gaping, bloody sockets in place of eyelids. The flesh continually shredded off in red gobbets . . ." Like Emma, we feel ourselves jolted from the lulling cadences of romantic reverie, the more so as the beggar is singing a little song: *"A clear day's warmth will often move / A lass to stray in dreams of love . . ."*

This is Flaubert's cunning game—to divide our inner loyalties. In the early pages he wins us to Emma, inching up on her dissatisfaction, her growing sense of entrapment; we dream along with her—who wouldn't? Her longings seem so fine and the texture of the provincial world around her so coarse. Then, gradually, by stages we readily understand, if not endorse, he draws us into the drama of her loves. Only later, and then slowly, does he show us the extent of her narcissistic mania. It is with Emma and us, in a sense, as it is with Emma and the merchant Lheureux, who by subtle maneuvering increases her debt to him at every turn. We scarcely know how far we are mortgaging ourselves to her, suspending our social judgments, falling in with her fantasies of rapturous love become permanent. Even late in the book, we are there with her in the carriage. We are full of foreboding, yes, but we are also sharing vicariously some of her afterglow.

The beggar, then, is not so much the reality principle as a figure from some moral counterworld in which excess is served back in its grotesquely inverted form. The reader shudders—the blind man is like a character out of Edgar Allan Poe, the afflicted host in "The Masque of the Red Death." Yet as he hobbles alongside the carriage, we also have the feeling that he is intimately bound to her. As he is, in the way that a shadow is bound to the shape it maps. If he is not her fate, he is the mocking commentary upon it. Indeed, as Flaubert finally contrives things, the beggar just happens to be passing on the sidewalk in Yonville at the very moment Emma is suffering her final death agony, and once again, he is singing his song of the lass straying in her dreams of love. Emma's last words are not to Charles, who hovers in anguish beside her. What she cries out in her ultimate spasm, after she has already hurled herself at the crucifix held out by the priest, imprinting on it, "with every ounce of her failing strength, the most passionate love-kiss she had ever given," as she is drawing her last racking breath what she cries out is "The blind man!"

But thankfully Emma's are not the book's last words. Flaubert took great pains to begin the novel with Charles, the gangling schoolboy with the preposterous hat, and in the end, as the lens draws away from the tragedy of Emma's suicide, he returns us to Charles, who is broken now by grief and looking for a way to carry on in the absence of his great love. He finally can't—in the end his pain breaks him. *Madame Bovary* closes with his death. Calm, quiet, unnoticed, his is a death in every way opposite to Emma's. And so the two stories, two fates, are folded together.

Better: Emma's explosive anguish is contained—we could say cushioned—by Charles's almost pathetic devotion, and her ravenous wanting is through some strange alchemy redeemed. When we finally shut the book we don't feel the terror and pity appropriate to high tragedy so much as the resonant sorrow that still honors the step-by-step continuity of life.

I marvel now at the interior distance these several readings seem to measure. How much of Flaubert's wisdom did I recognize back in the bunkhouse in Deer Lodge, Montana, in the summer of 1971? I knew so little of love, what coiled springs of joy and despair are packed down inside that one all-purpose concept. I had so little inkling about the tolls we pay on our inescapably grandiose fantasies, or how cruelly the loss of love can strip us back to our most basic foundations. That was all to come. I was naïve about compulsion and mostly ignorant of the torments of jealousy. But even so I read and I was moved. Moreover, every time since then I have been moved anew, but in different ways and for different reasons. And I have never had the feeling with *Madame Bovary* that I've had with so many other books, of sometimes touching bottom as I read.

This would be my personal test for the ultimate artistic greatness of a work—whether having read it I am drawn back, over time, to read it again, and, no less important, whether on return I feel, like any prodigal, the heartsick melting sensation that the first glimpse of home so often delivers. *Bovary,* taken in at first so reluctantly, has become, one of my few solid points of reference, persuading me that Flaubert had it right, that there can be an ideal alignment of words and sentences.

The Mad Energies of Art

Saul Bellow's *Humboldt's Gift*

W HENEVER SOMEONE asks me to name my favorite novel, I find myself putting on a ridiculous but revealing little performance. I pretend to a natural consternation—after all, who can narrow a lifetime's evolving preferences down to a single title?—but I use that as a cover for the real calculation, which is whether I have the interest or energy to explain my choice. For in fact I do have a favorite novel—*Humboldt's Gift* by Saul Bellow—but I know it to be an eccentric work, one that a number of reputable critics had problems with when it was published, and that many intelligent readers I know have shaken their heads over. How much easier to cite *Under the Volcano,* or *The Portrait of a Lady,* or *Ulysses,* or *To the Lighthouse,* all works that I admire without reservation. But the question was *favorite* novel, which novel I visit most often in my thoughts, know most intimately, down to the structure of its cadences, and which fills me with the greatest covetousness *and* inspires me to emulation. This is my truest test: when I think of *Humboldt's Gift* I immediately want to write.

They say that love is blind, but I don't agree. Love is often well aware of the flaws of the beloved—but love is love because it overrules the fault-finding impulse altogether in the name of . . . in the name of a flow of higher sympathy that feels like an end in itself. I love *Humboldt's Gift*—much as anyone can love a book—and my love is unperturbed by all that my judging intellect whispers as I read: that it is structurally lopsided, overwrought in its Rudolf Steiner–inspired meditations, improbable in its *deus ex machina* resolutions. I grant that there are problems and short-comings, but they don't ruffle my devotion at all.

I can bring back my first reading of *Humboldt's Gift* with an exaggerated vividness, though I can't recall how the book came into my possession. I mention this little snag because I know that my copy was a new hardcover—the cover price an even $10—and because this was a period in my life when I was routinely counting the change spread out on the dresser top. I would never have paid full price in a bookstore. Was it a birthday gift? That makes sense because my birthday is in late September, and I read the novel first in October of 1975 in a single great gulp. And *this* I remember because it was the most desperate season in my life so far, and because for a long time after I credited Saul Bellow with helping to save me from a descent into utter hopelessness.

The previous August I had ended what had until then been the big romantic relationship of my life. I had left our life in Maine and returned broke and empty-handed to my old haunts in Ann Arbor, where I had gone to college a few years before. I'd been back in town for some weeks, and whatever plan I had for rebuilding my life was not working. Although I had rented a small room and had a job in a bookstore, these were not support enough. I would wake up each day deeply depressed, wondering how I would make it through to the next. My sadness was overwhelming. I had no one except my sister to confide in, and nothing at all to hold against my thoughts of "never again." One afternoon I snapped. I had to do something, I made the impulsive (and ultimately foolish) decision to borrow money from a friend and fly to Boston the next morning. There I would board the first bus north. Although I had no idea of what I might do, or even of what I was after, once I'd decided there was no other choice. There was only the rest of the day and the night to get through.

In my room, a shabby attic box high up among the treetops, I paced and kneaded my hands like some latter-day Raskolnikov. I was beside myself, twitching in my skin. I had no idea how I would pass the time. And then—I can't remember why—from among the handful of books I had stacked up on my dresser, I took down *Humboldt's Gift* and, given my state, against all odds read. I turned the pages through the late afternoon and the evening, and then on through the night. I read as I'd never read anything before, with a lock-on fury that pushed the world and my extraordinary anxiety aside. At first it was to get away from my situation, but then at some point that shifted, and I was reading to get further and further in. I didn't finish the whole book that night—it's a long novel. But I immersed myself so deeply in the narrative of Charlie Citrine's fate that I awakened, by reader's proxy—that sympathetic magic that sometimes happens between story and self—my own sense of fatedness, and that sense was there in me at every moment in the next days as I walked up and down the roads outside Kennebunkport and blundered through the finale of the relationship that had been everything to me.

About that night I remember several things. I remember the narrow spring-shot bed that was part of the punishment of that room, that season, and how I arranged myself there, propped up in a corner, scarcely aware of the discomfort, mainly glad that I was able to rig the desk lamp on the chair to get the right lighting. And, contents aside—for Bellow's writing impressed itself on me with a once-in-a-lifetime clarity—I remember the physical book, the cover and the feel of the pages, pulpier than any paper I'd felt before in a trade hardcover. This anomaly somehow became linked in my mind with the eccentric novelty of Bellow's plot, underscoring the feeling that this was not just another novel, but an advance posting of imminent changes in the literary life of our times.

We never know, do we, if the future is just more of the present pushed forward, or whether the look and feel, not to mention the fundamental essence, of life might not be changing? This is part of the galvanizing horror—and thrill—of great disasters, too: the possibility that the great change might have at last begun. I subscribed for a long time to the idea that artists and writers were, as Pound had said, our antennae, and that if news of transformation were to come, it would be through the channels they created. When I read *Humboldt's Gift,* keyed-up, holding on tight through my own private torment, I felt that something very new and important was being delivered. Bellow had achieved that level of seeing where lives could be viewed without derision as destinies; he had given me a glimpse of a larger system of meaning that I could incorporate into my own life. And he had done it in a way that felt of the moment, contemporary.

I didn't recognize all of this directly, of course. I experienced it as I experience much of what I read—as atmosphere, as tone, as a stirring up of suppositions and surmises, as a kind of extended daydream. But the transforming gaze of hindsight now tells me that it was there from the start, drawn—all of it—like electricity through the circuit of the opening passage:

The book of ballads published by Von Humboldt Fleisher in the Thirties was an immediate hit. Humboldt was just what everyone had been waiting for. Out in the Midwest I had certainly been waiting eagerly, I can tell you that. An avant-garde writer, the first of a new generation, he was handsome, fair, large, serious, witty, he was learned. The guy had it all. All the papers reviewed his book. His picture appeared in *Time* without insult and in *Newsweek* with praise. I read *Harlequin Ballads* enthusiastically. I was a student at the University of Wisconsin and thought about nothing but literature day and night. Humboldt revealed to me new ways of doing things. I was ecstatic. I envied his luck, his talent, and his fame, and I went east in May to have a look at him—perhaps to get next to him. The Greyhound bus, taking the Scranton route, made the trip in about fifty hours. That didn't matter. The bus windows were open. I had never seen real mountains before. Trees were budding. It was like Beethoven's *Pastorale.* I felt showered by the green within. Manhattan was fine, too. I took a room for three bucks a week and found a job selling Fuller Brushes door to door. And I was wildly excited about everything. Having written Humboldt a long fan letter, I was invited to Greenwich Village to discuss literature and ideas. He lived on Bedford Street, near Chumley's. First he gave me black coffee, and then poured gin in the same cup. "Well, you're a nice-looking enough fellow, Charlie," he said to me. "Aren't you a bit sly, maybe? I think you're headed for early baldness. And such large emotional handsome eyes. But you certainly do love literature and that's the main thing. You have sensibility," he said. He was a pioneer in the use of this word. Sensibility later made it big. Humboldt was very kind. He introduced me to people in the Village and got me books to review. I always loved him.

The pull of the prose was irresistible. I loved the velocity, the declarative forthrightness, the apparent ease with which Bellow nailed the urgency of literary adoration, a vice to which I was highly susceptible back in my middle twenties, and which I have only very slowly, and still not completely, outgrown—writers were my rock stars, and I followed their doings with a fetishistic zeal. But beyond the narrator's adoration was something more potent still—his absolute certainty that this business of poetry and writing and publishing mattered, that it was the sovereign real thing.

Humboldt's Gift is a baggy, talky book, crammed with episodic set pieces—comic as well as elegiac interludes—but the gist of the narration is as follows. Charlie Citrine, the man pegged early on as having "sensibility," is in Chicago fumbling through what is thankfully never called a "midlife crisis," but which bears all of the now clichéd markings of that disorder. A successful thinker and man of letters (he has two Pulitzers under his belt), Charlie finds himself in his midfifties assailed from all sides as well as from within. His ex-wife, Denise, has her cutthroat lawyers after him for a fat divorce settlement; his sensuously manipulative younger girlfriend, Renata, is trying to get him to go with her to Madrid, with some idea that she will reconnect with her long-lost father and marry Charlie. Moreover, his beloved Mercedes Benz has just been pulverized by a bat-wielding hood named Rinaldo Cantabile, who claims that Charlie welshed on paying a poker debt and who now insists on restitution.

At the same time, more centrally, Charlie, an amateur student of the anthroposophy of Rudolf Steiner (premised on the possibility of the attainment of ever-higher states of spiritual consciousness), has begun to experience vivid memories of the eponymous Humboldt, the great friend of his young manhood, the poet—supposedly based on the poet Delmore Schwartz—who went down to pills, alcohol, and dementia in his own middle years. Charlie now feels guilty; he feels that he might have abandoned Humboldt in his time of greatest suffering.

The novel becomes a self-accounting on every level, its various plot strands drawn together, its elements put into play, by the revelation that a legacy of sorts left by Humboldt has turned up. How Bellow manages to orchestrate everything is hard to discover, even when the pieces are all lined up for study, but then this has always been Bellow's particular art—creating a narrative voice so rich and suggestive, so fluid in its movements between past and present, that the plod of sequential development is avoided altogether. There is the feeling when reading this novel that a tightly rolled sultan's carpet has splashed open before our eyes with one swift nudge of the foot.

I have read *Humboldt's Gift* four or five times now and each time it tunes me up differently, not to the point where I would say it's a new novel—for the sense of deep familiarity remains for me one of its magnetic attractions—but in terms of offering me vital new information. That's the kind of book it is, and don't we all have them—books we reread not for any purpose of overt self-betterment, not to add to our trophy bag, but because they nourish us with clues about the nature of life as we try to solve it for ourselves?

Lying in that poor man's bed in that tiny upstairs room that night, threading the sentences end to end with fervid fixation, I took two major kinds of solace from my reading. The first, as I already suggested, was the solace of literature mattering, this in spite of the fact that literature—writing—does not in the end save either Humboldt, who for all his literary wisdom went down in flames, consumed by his demons, or Charlie, who never does make headway on his great projected study of boredom. Even so, the intoxication Bellow creates in the opening sections is so powerful, so triumphantly idealized, that it is—to crib from Joseph Brodsky's "Roman Elegies"—"enough to last the whole blackout." Page after page we are lifted by a mighty swell as Bellow does what he does best of all: summoning the passion of the mind for ideas and expressions of beauty. He does it by the main force of enthusiasm, with lists, little symphonic surges of reference, evoking through his rhythms the very excitement he is bent on conveying.

But Bellow doesn't just rely on the cumulative power of the catalogue. He creates the surrounding atmosphere—the *mise en scène*—and invites us into the life of the moment, sharpening our sense of the pressure of intellect and sensibility on his various characters.

In one of his early Chicago reveries (he is hiding from the world for the morning, meditating on Humboldt), Charlie recalls a visit he paid to Humboldt and his wife Kathleen when they lived in rural New Jersey. He captures the manic chaos of the drive out, leaving New York with the poet at the wheel of his old Buick. "Steering, he was humped huge over the wheel, he had small-boy tremors of the hands and feet, and he kept the cigarette holder between his teeth. He was agitated, talking away, entertaining, provoking, informing, and snowing me." And: "We were off: he discussed machinery, luxury, command, capitalism, technology, Mammon, Orpheus and poetry, the riches of the human heart, America, world civilization. His task was to put all of this, and more, together. The car went snoring and squealing through the tunnel and came out in bright sunlight."

Then they arrive: "Briars lashed the Roadmaster as we swayed on huge springs through rubbishy fields where white boulders sat. The busted muffler was so loud that though the car filled the lane there was no need to honk. You could hear us coming. Humboldt yelled, "Here's our place!" and swerved. We rolled over a hummock or earth-wave. The front of the Buick rose and then dived into the weeds."

And so it goes, the most vividly deployed scene-making setting us up for the gush of his enthusiasm, which I excerpt midflow lest the pages-long hammering overwhelm everything else:

About Eliot he seemed to know strange facts no one else had ever heard. He was filled with gossip and hallucination as well as literary theory. Distortion was inherent, yes, in all poetry. But which came first? And this rained down on me, part privilege, part pain, with illustrations from the classics and the sayings of Einstein and Zsa Zsa Gabor, with references to Polish socialism and the football tactics of George Halas and the secret motives of Arnold Toynbee, and (somehow) the used-car business. Rich boys, poor

boys, jewboys, chorus girls, prostitution and religion, old money,
new money, gentlemen's clubs, Back Bay, Newport, Washington
Square, Henry Adams, Henry James, Henry Ford, Saint John of
the Cross, Dante, Ezra Pound, Dostoevski, Marilyn Monroe and
Joe DiMaggio, Gertrude Stein and Alice, Freud and Ferenczi.

The early pages of *Humboldt's Gift* offer a supercharged saturation of
this heady referential narrative. Remembering his great doomed friend,
Charlie recreates in the rhythm of his thoughts the sensation of the very
mania that brought Humboldt down. To me, a confused, intellectually
ambitious twenty-four-year-old, it was like a drug. Even in my tormented
state, my reading brought me to a pitch of wanting. This was it—the life
of the mind, the re-creation of what brilliance felt like. Bellow was not
giving us the isolated facts and concepts—the slow contents of the books
I studied. Here was the payoff, evidence of how a powerful mind took
hold of the world, turning the rough givens of circumstance into intense
comprehension. I could feel how the world was remade into meaning,
and I believed then that there was no higher use to which the responsive
psyche could be put.

I'd had my own glimpses of this fever, but at a much lower level. I'd already put in a few seasons working in bookstores, falling into bookseller's
psychosis, those associative fugues in which every page I scanned somehow related to something else I'd just been reading. Night after night I'd
made my way home from the store with stacks of borrowed books in bags,
frustrated that I could only follow one path at a time, wishing for some
Faustian pill that would confer on me the instant mastery I craved, even
at the price of . . . well, I had nothing much to offer up in trade.

Bellow's Humboldt passages lit all of this up in me, that night as later,
removing me from the immediate burn of my romantic obsession, in part
through my absorption in the writing, but also by drawing the energies of
one obsession temporarily into another. From the exalted vantage offered by
Humboldt's intellect—a vantage comprehending history, poetry, politics—
my heartbroken condition seemed consolingly small potatoes. The problem
with these easily acquired perspectives is that they don't last long once the
book is closed. When I finally found my way back to Kennebunkport, hik-

ing and hitching from place to place, those aerial-view consolations were not enough.

Later, though, once I was home and licking my wounds, finishing the book, I experienced the late-breaking balm of commiseration. This was the gift of the book's later chapters, the second solace, and it gave me a way to join Bellow's narrative to my own heartache. In the novel, Charlie has gone with Renata to Europe. He has not done the right thing, has not offered to make her an honest woman. Now, suddenly—to him, shockingly—Renata has disappeared. She has stranded him in Madrid with her elderly mother, the scheming Señora, and her young son. Charlie is stunned, bereft. "Good-by, good-by to those wonderful sensations," he thinks. "Mine at least had been the real thing. And if hers were not, she had at least been a true and understanding pal. In her percale bed. In her heaven of piled pillows. All that was probably over."

It is. The news arrives while Charlie is still in Madrid. Renata has married his rival, the mortuary king Flonzaley. Charlie goes into a precipitous decline. At one point, he imagines how he must look to others in the *pensione* he has retired to: "His brown eyes were red from weeping, he dressed with high elegance although the kitchen smells made his clothing noticeably rancid, he tried with persistent vanity to comb his thin and graying hair over the bald middle of his head and was always disheartened when he realized that in the lamplight his scalp was glistening."

Oh the sadness and indignity of life! What a bond I felt, pushing through the later pages of the novel in the wake of my failure. In Charlie's abandonment I saw my own. No matter. The absence he felt touched the absence I felt, and between fiction and life there passed a sense of the Virgilian "tears of things" that fortified me, allowing me to admit my grief and at the same time to hold it as in a frame. And when I finally finished, seeing Charlie through to his hard-won acceptance, to his redemptive moment of laying his ghosts to rest and pushing on, I felt subtly altered.

I find this whole transaction fascinating, how in reading I experience the emotional situations created by the author, and how these scenarios play on my own sensibility, sometimes so intensely that I experience an actual physical agitation, a kind of shortness of breath of the whole being. How much of this, I wonder, is a function of the author's art, the formal tension of scene-making and the sentence-by-sentence creation of the feeling-states of the characters, and how much has to do with the intensity of my own projected emotions? To what degree was I filling in Charlie's sense of loss with my own?

My guess now, after my most recent re-reading, is that it was quite a bit. Now that so much time had passed, and so much of the hurt had been absorbed by the system, I could feel the differential. This time it was the quality of the prose, the writerly characterization—the identifications I provided were more rooted in memory than visceral immediacy. Still moved, I was not as devastated as I had been. Of course, I was reading a novel that has become familiar; I knew in advance that Charlie would get past his grief. My focus—now as in earlier re-readings—was on other things.

At some point after this first encounter, *Humboldt's Gift* took on a somewhat different significance for me. It became a literary model, a work I nearly fetishized for its voice and narrative energy, for its human reach. Bellow, I thought, had cracked the code. Almost alone among contemporary novelists, he had found a way to show the complexity of our way of living without losing the contemplative register or sacrificing the full emotional spectrum. He could be, as the situation required, philosophical, comedic, descriptively evocative, elegiac, dramatic—and he could get in close to the endless psychological push-pull of relationships, the tenderness and leveraging manipulation of lovers, the *odi et amo* of embattled friendships. I was enraptured by Bellow's scenes and, even more specifically, his prose. So many moments spoke to me *exactly*. Whole long runs of his sentences fired me with the desire to write, but at the same time filled me with the despairing thought that I could never do as well, though it is the hubris of every young writer to imagine that all obstacles to greatness will be overcome in the indeterminate future.

I'll let a single passage showcase the prose for me. Here is Charlie, describing the clientele of the old Russian Bathhouse:

These Division Street steam-bathers don't look like the trim proud people downtown. Even old Feldstein pumping his Exercycle in the Downtown Club at the age of eighty would be out of place on Division Street. Forty years ago Feldstein was a swinger, a high roller, a good-time Charlie on Rush Street. In spite of his age he is a man of today, whereas the patrons of the Russian Bath are cast in an antique form. They have swelling buttocks and fatty breasts as yellow as buttermilk. They stand on thick pillar legs affected with a sort of creeping verdigris or blue-cheese mottling of the ankles. After steaming, these old fellows eat enormous snacks of bread and salt herring or large ovals of salami and dripping skirt-steak and they drink schnapps. They could knock down walls with their hard stout old-fashioned bellies. Things are very elementary here. You feel that these people are almost conscious of obsolescence, of a line of evolution abandoned by nature and culture. So down in the super-heated subcellars all these Slavonic cavemen and wood demons with hanging laps of fat and legs of stone and lichen boil themselves and splash ice water on their heads by the bucket. Upstairs, on the television screen in the locker room, little dudes and grinning broads make smart talk or leap up and down. They are unheeded. Mickey who keeps the food concession fries slabs of meat and potato pancakes, and, with enormous knives, he hacks up cabbages for coleslaw and he quarters grapefruits (to be eaten by hand). The stout old men mounting in their bed sheets from the blasting heat have a strong appetite.

This is more than just a bravura description. Any good sense-attuned writer could have put together the details. What makes the passage stand out for me is the deep, almost primal regard—the love, the awe—Bellow transmits. We feel, through Charlie, that we are spying on history—our ancestors' ancestors caught in full-flesh. How does he manage everything at once, the grotesque excess, the atmosphere, the charged analogies? There is always a mystery with great writing, how is one thing brought to combine with another? I often have the sense while reading Bellow that he is not just giving us a scene, a conjuring of people in a place, but something closer to a philosophy. Charlie's particular regard can be taken without much stretch as a reflection on the ontological fitness of what Irving

Howe called "the world of our fathers." These staggering old troglodytes are, in Charlie's vision of things—a vision we have by this point become immersed in—set against the new, the young, the modern ("Upstairs, on the television screen in the locker room, little dudes and grinning broads make smart talk or leap up and down."), and if they are a physical shambles with their fatty old breasts, they are yet a force of superior denomination. They are—so I read it—closer to fundamental *being*.

And then there is the voice, Charlie's wonderful—and nearly simultaneous—command of registers, how he can swerve from the wise-guy voice ("dudes" and "broads") to the reflective ("these people are almost conscious of obsolescence"), to the overtly literary-descriptive ("They stand on thick pillar legs affected with a sort of creeping verdigris") and pull it off.

Although I envy more than a few writers, coveting this one's fluency, that one's exactitude, I am seldom provoked to outright emulation. *The Catcher in the Rye* had that effect, I remember, and *Lolita,* but no novel affected me in the way that *Humboldt's Gift* did, especially in my younger years. The mere contemplation of the Bellovian sweep would rouse my ambition. I wanted badly to write a novel of equal range and texture, alive down to its least bit character, a novel able to transmit the drama of the inner life even as it staged episodes from the human comedy and registered in its smallest inflection the tone of our times. I sat long hours straining to dream up the perfect opening, the sentence that would seem as electric and inevitable as Bellow's beautifully simple: "The book of ballads published by Von Humboldt Fleisher in the Thirties was an immediate hit." It was not to be. I did not understand that the perfect sentence is not a happy accident, but something more like a consummation, an announcement that everything—the whole work—is in place, ready.

I WANT TO STAY NEAR this business of voice, the particular spanning of outer and inner that Bellow has fashioned to such a high art. For the voice was a big part of what so affected me in my most recent reading of the novel. Indeed, this time through I was less caught up in the tragedy of Humboldt, or the comedic Chicago set pieces, or even the romantic travails that were so piercing to me the first time. Older, I was most taken with Bellow's rendering of Charlie as a man floundering in time, a man in search of the larger synthesis.

In my earlier readings of the novel I missed the importance of the fact that Charlie was a middle-aged man not just living his life, but even more significantly, re-living it. But this is—I would say *mercifully*—the blindness of youth. Young, we cut the cloth of the world to our own feelings and understandings. To me, back then, Charlie was, as had been Emma Bovary before him, just an adult of indeterminate adult status. I had no way of grasping him otherwise. I hadn't, certainly when I was first reading *Humboldt*, experienced the wonderful and terrible ways in which as we get older the film of our own lives increasingly doubles over on itself, returning us to things we had thought safely buried, recirculating old poisons, throwing the glare of hindsight down onto choices made . . . Well, now I know. And this time in my reading it clicked for me. I grasped—felt—the extent to which the work is—and I don't think the comparison is that far-fetched—Bellow's *Inferno*. Charlie is a man awakening to himself in the middle of a dark wood and finding that the straight way has become lost. Where Dante is allegorical, Bellow is often hammy and oblique, full of comic and ironic impulses. But the overall feeling of the work is still one of often sorrowful retrospection. And the ultimate thrust is transformational—the point is to show us a man who goes into his darkness to wrestle his devils, and who finally comes through.

The core confrontation is, of course, with memories of his younger self, especially of his friendship with Humboldt and what he must face there: his own egotism, his fear of the decline and failure Humboldt represented, and the fact that he deserted the poet in his time of need. The relationship is complex, and Humboldt from his side acted unpardonably toward Charlie, taking advantage of his loyalty in a dozen different ways. That Humboldt drifted in and out of delusion only partially exonerates him. Charlie had good reasons for pulling away from his friend in the end.

But these reasons and explanations only satisfy on the psychological plane. Charlie in middle age is determined to break through to a higher spiritual apprehension of things, and from his new vantage—when he can attain it—he sees the past very differently. Tormenting and manipulative as his friend was, he was also, over and above that, a radiant spirit, a man of soul dreaming his way toward the original world: "Ah Humboldt had been great," thinks Charlie, "handsome, high-spirited, buoyant, ingenious, electrical, noble. To be with him made you feel the sweetness of life. We used to discuss the loftiest things—what Diotima said to Socrates about love, what Spinoza meant by *amor dei intellectualis.* To talk to him was sustaining, nourishing." In the light of this recognition, Charlie has come up seriously short in his self-accounting. When, toward the end of the poet's life, Charlie spotted him standing in shambles on a street corner, eating a "dusty" pretzel, he turned away. For this he cannot forgive himself.

It is the intensity of his remorse, perhaps, that lets Charlie stage the scenes of their early friendship with such piercing clarity. The memories of Humboldt carry the first part of the book. At the same time, they establish the vibrant inwardness of Charlie in middle age and make plausible his aspirations toward—as the title of his master Rudolf Steiner's book would have it—*Knowledge of the Higher Worlds and Its Attainment.*

Charlie's (and Bellow's) insistent mysticism, the repeated invocation of Steiner, his teachings and spiritual exercises, confounded critics and reviewers when the book first appeared. The novel was seen to be full of crackpot excess and distended metaphysical passages. I see them differently. Plucking from one of these almost at random, I find:

For in spirit, says Steiner, a man can step out of himself and let things speak to him about themselves, to speak about what has meaning not for him alone but also for them. Thus the sun the moon the stars will speak to nonastronomers in spite of their ignorance of science. In fact it's high time that this happened. Ignorance of science should not keep one imprisoned in the lowest and weariest sector of being, prohibited from entering into independent relations with the creation as a whole. The educated speak of the disenchanted (a boring) world. But it is not the world, it is my own head that is disenchanted. The world *cannot* be disenchanted.

It's true, some of Charlie's anthroposophical riffs go on too long, straining the already loosely carpentered structure of the novel. But I don't mind in the least. The truth is that I spend much of my life egging myself closer to the ledge—to some more open recognition of forces beyond what we usually credit in our ordinary day. I torment myself with the possibility that there might indeed be planes of higher meaning, available syntheses. Part of the enormous appeal of this novel for me is that a writer as gifted and intelligent as Bellow shows himself unapologetically interested in this very thing. What a man to have on the team. What a ratification!

This appetite is not new. When I was much younger it pulled me toward Walt Whitman (briefly), or, differently, D. H. Lawrence; later there was Rainer Maria Rilke. Even so, I remember in my early readings of the novel being impatient, wanting to get past these pages to get to scenes and more sensory passages. But this time I lingered, savoring. For passing time has taught me about the undertow power of memory, it has also made me very keen to learn how the outer man can in all the situations of life draw on his inwardness, and not just in the interest of greater understanding, or for solace. There is a larger wisdom to be drawn from Charlie's obsession—which is to say from Bellow's vision—and that is the idea that contact with our deeper intuitions might actually reposition us in whatever situation we are in *and* thus change the situation—the Heisenberg uncertainty principle borrowed from scientific experiment and applied to living itself. Changed awareness can actually affect the way things happen; dropping certain resistances and defenses alters the terms of encounter.

Obviously there is no way to argue this coherently, certainly no way to prove it, but I will say that of all of the novel's many features, the most striking for me now was the sense Bellow conveyed of experience unfolding with larger thematic inflection. He could only achieve this rare effect because he had created in Charlie Citrine a character deeply attuned to these thematic surges. In a sense the whole point of the novel, at one level, is Charlie's recognition of this movement of meaning and his eventual giving over to it. When he does—when he gives up the Renata struggle in Madrid, and accepts his character, and his responsibility for all that has happened to him—I experience a great sense of lifting free. Charlie has come

through—he has come to terms with the demons of his own character—
and if he does not look up at the end to glimpse, as did Dante, the stars,
he does make the decision to rebury his old friend Humboldt (literally
and figuratively) and on leaving the cemetery he makes a significant pause
to identify a budding crocus under last autumn's leaves.

I won't pretend that I have tapped fully the many wisdoms of Bellow's
book or brought them into my life, but time has done its steady work,
and I do feel, more than ever before, that I can recognize how these understandings and intuitions have their place. It's too early, yet—for me, as
indeed for Charlie—to claim with any certainty that there are actually
higher worlds to be entered. None of us may ever know for sure. But I
will say that the reading of the novel, the imaginative projection that it
asks, filled the days with a thematic resonance that seemed to be my own
life—and past—vibrating in direct sympathy with the life on the page.
Humboldt's Gift is my "favorite" book because it keeps renewing itself for
me as I get older, outpacing me in a way that makes me speed my step.

The Murderer's Fancy Prose Style

Vladimir Nabokov's *Lolita*

IN CREATING A SYLLABUS for my broadly defined course in "Writing about the Arts," I had one of those lowercase brainstorms that I hope for every teaching season. I thought I would combine a reading of Vladimir Nabokov's *Lolita,* one of the small handful of novels I can return to endlessly, with a study of Azar Nafisi's *Reading Lolita in Tehran,* which I'd seen reviewed everywhere a few months before. The Nafisi had just the sort of topical currency that I thought would help lay to rest any suspicion that I was just looking to smuggle lubricious materials into my Mt. Holyoke classroom under the guise of "art." To throw another genre into the mix, I would offer a classroom screening of Adrian Lyne's then-recent—and somewhat controversial—film *Lolita.* An interesting range of exposures—no question. But I was brewing more business than that. I imagined that the novel would prove combustible enough in the dominantly female Mt. Holyoke classroom to help me fire up an essay I would then call "Reading *Lolita* in South Hadley," an of-the-moment reflection on this most disconcertingly appealing of novels.

But my students subverted my expectation immediately. Not by approving or trivializing anything Humbert did or confided—they were all properly disturbed (only one of fourteen had read the novel before)—but by overruling that response with another. Simply: they declared themselves entranced with Humbert's mind and the beauty and originality of his—that is to say, Nabokov's—language. One after the next, with an enthusiasm I rarely find in these student/book encounters, they remarked on his wit, his beautiful phrases, his images, his elaborate references, and the astonishing precision of his prose. In fact, not only did Humbert Humbert capture their imaginations—with fascination and pity—but he did so in spite of their powerful (and stated) predisposition to pronounce him guilty. They were hardly blind to his monstrosity, but even though I felt that many of them wanted to condemn the deeds as well as the sensibility that had conjured them up, they couldn't quite do it. Their feelings had sheered off from their moral judgments. They were, I could see, dismayed to encounter so directly the confusing power of art. And this seems to me, in our or any age, a remarkable thing—a vote not just for the claims of an exacerbated sensibility, but also for the allusive, ironic, romantic detail-encrusted prose that would press those claims.

So yes, my envisioned project—all about testing the moral reflexes of a generation of young women—while not derailed, was shunted onto a new track. I was sent, in cartoon parlance, "back to the drawing board." But what I discovered was that I was far from disappointed by the change. If anything, I was heartened, for I was finally able to admit that it has never been the "scandalous" aspect of *Lolita* that interests me. What I've always been drawn to is its complex presentation of romantic obsession, the wonderfully paradoxical fact that the comedy, scored throughout, does not undermine the ultimate pathos of the story, but even intensifies it.

Nabokov explores this romantic mania as though it were his mission on earth to do so, and in his intensity he nails it. The confessions of Humbert Humbert confirm each of us in our most private flights of madness. I'll risk the generalization. We don't need to be pedophiles to relate to it; we only need to have at some point in our lives been fixated on another person. And it's these most vulnerable states, along with our safeguarded secrets, that we draw on to bring Humbert Humbert's compulsion—with its cunning ploys, paranoid jealousies, and delicious imaginings—to its fullest life.

Reading Humbert Humbert's account of lying awake in bed that first night at *The Enchanted Hunters* inn, for example, I tune in to the antennae-waving hesitation with which he traverses the acreage of inches that separates him from his sleeping prey, and I am completely with him. But I'm pulled along by more than just the suspense of the prose. In the suddenly lit-up theater of memory, I'm a fourteen-year-old boy again, spending my last night at a Latvian summer camp in the woods of Michigan. For some reason I no longer remember, a whole group of us, boys and girls, are sleeping together in a mass on the floor of a large communal cabin. Although ostensibly separated by our disaffected counselors, we've managed under cover of dark to cross boundaries and mix things up, creating all kinds of possibilities for adjacency. And in all of this surreptitious inch-worming of sleeping bags I've worked it so that I am no more than a foot away from a girl named Sigrid. I knew, as one always knows, that Sigrid didn't really *like* me in the way I liked her, but she didn't give any signs of *dis*liking me, and somehow this allowed me to make my scratchy way over to her. I was like the arrow in Zeno's paradox, subdividing each distance until arrival seemed impossible. Except I did at last arrive. What's more, Sigrid not only seemed to know what was happening, but by careful degrees she adjusted her own position so that somewhere near dawn I could come up against her backside "spoon" fashion. And there I lay, who knows how long, taking the highest possible pleasure from the lightest possible pressure (a sleeping bag is the ultimate prophylactic). Everything I had stored but forgotten from that experience was alive again when I read how Humbert Humbert's "tentacles moved towards her again," and how he finally got himself so close to his drugged prey that he "felt the aura of her bare shoulder like a warm breath" on his cheek.

But I'm getting carried away by my own tendency to Humbertize— to magnify the dynamics of certain sensations out of all proportion and to fetishize details. My point was just that Humbert Humbert's oh-so-specifically directed energies found echoing corroboration in a memory I'd forgotten. But then, almost everything in the novel seems so familiar. I even felt a heart-pounding kinship with the man as he plotted out just what steps he would take to drown the dreary Charlotte Haze and make the death look accidental. Of course, I have never myself schemed, except in my idlest fantasies, how to actually do away with someone—not in Nabokovian detail, anyway—but Humbert Humbert's obsessive factoring of every possibility had me thinking like a would-be killer. And it seemed very familiar, as if it were all there right on tap. But maybe there is a less self-indicting explanation. Maybe the cunning and heartlessness I thrilled to in his imagining are the same that I tap into day in and day out as I conduct my psychological assaults on my friends and neighbors, though of course the latter are on a proportionately much smaller scale.

But reader identification has to be secondary to other things. I really wanted—here, as in my writing class—to honor the spirit of first things first, and with *Lolita* the first of all things has to be Nabokov's fabulous prose, which in a matter of a few all-but-immortal sentences ravishes us—a condition from which we never recover for the duration of the reading—even as we know our ravishment is but a pale version of what Humbert Humbert felt early in the book when he stepped onto Charlotte Haze's "piazza," at which point, as he writes: "without the least warning, a blue sea-wave swelled under my heart and, from a mat in a pool of sun, half-naked, kneeling, turning about on her knees, there was my Riviera love peering at me over dark glasses." It is, of course, Lolita, she of the celebrated opening invocation:

> Lolita, light of my life, fire of my loins. My sin, my soul, Lo-lee-ta: the tip of the tongue taking a trip of three steps down the palate to tap, at three, on the teeth. Lo. Lee. Ta.
>
> She was Lo, plain Lo, in the morning, standing four feet ten in one sock. She was Lola in slacks. She was Dolly at school. She was Dolores on the dotted line. But in my arms she was always Lolita.
>
> Did she have a precursor? She did, indeed she did. In point of fact, there might have been no Lolita at all had I not loved, one summer, a certain initial girl-child. In a princedom by the sea.

Already in these two moments we have a first approach to the mystery of Humbert Humbert and the novel as well as an occasion to remark on the extraordinary importance of openings. Say what you will, the impression we take from these first sentences of Humbert Humbert's "memoir" is so strong and persuasive, so *winning* at the deepest possible level, that we carry it before us like the pilgrim carried the sign of the cross into the

land of the infidel—except that it is our very own narrator and protagonist whose deeper nature we would arm ourselves against.

These first words strike up a blaze of love that is never quenched, not
even by the lowest and most self-serving of his revelations—love so strong
it has turned itself into radiant prose. But here is the trick, the catch.
For *Lolita* to work its full magic on us, we must also for a long stretch
forget that above and beyond anything else Humbert Humbert loves his
"Lo." We have to believe for long chapters that he is the most cunning
of perverts, a man on a quest for a strange aesthetic/erotic bliss. But why
would Nabokov plant the suggestion at all? Why not have us believe from
the start that we are in the grip of a pervert's elaborate self-accounting
and nothing more? Because, I'll argue, were he to do this we would then
have to see Humbert Humbert as irretrievably fallen. He would be too
cut off from the power that finally redeems him (though not his actions).
Nabokov understands that his narrator needs to move around in a cloud
of ambiguities so that he can keep fending off our typecasting impulses.
At the same time, he needs to leave in his reader whatever is the opposite
of a "shadow of doubt"—that slight suspicion of the positive, the intrinsi-
cally noble—which keeps us holding our breath for him.

And this the opening achieves. Not by insistence, and not through
the assertion of any upright moral impulse, but through rhythm and dic-
tion. Those sentences—alliterative, staccato, playful to the point of self-
delighted braggadocio—announce a purely joyous devotion. They invoke
nothing so much as the heedless muttered endearments that come after
lovemaking and that testify in their sportiveness to a complete trust, an
absolute giving over of the self. They are the effect that posits love and
tenderness as its immediate cause, and as such they predispose us deeply,
subliminally, to side with Humbert Humbert's passion, even as so much
of what we learn soon after provokes us in the other direction.

"You can always count on a murderer for a fancy prose style," writes
Humbert Humbert a few sentences on, and we are so busy shaking our
heads over the preposterous archness of the assertion that we almost miss
what he is telling us: he has killed someone; the very same man who can
suggest his blissful adoration with words—"the tip of the tongue taking a

trip . . ."—was capable of tugging a trigger. Eros, Thanatos. Welcome to Nabokov's world of contradictions, happy stalking ground for would-be psychologists.

Nabokov openly declared his scorn for the Freudian explanation of human behavior, a scorn that did not stop him from premising the origins of Humbert Humbert's mania on an uncharacteristically simplistic psychological scenario. To my mind, this is the least persuasive of the author's many artifices—Humbert Humbert's backstory: how when he was a mere boy, a young Edgar Poe, growing up near the Mediterranean, he loved a young girl, his Annabel Leigh (!), and how his initially innocent desire for her built over time to a pitch, leading him to the very brink of his first sexual experience. But at the crucial moment his tryst was interrupted and no second chances were offered. Annabel was taken away and reportedly died soon after, afflicting the young Humbert Humbert with a kind of amatory post-traumatic stress disorder. This we might define as an erotic trauma so profound as to instigate a lifelong "repetition compulsion," a pattern of deliberate, if subliminal, reenactments of the source experience, the drive being to master the situation once and for all and be rid of it.

It is a remarkable moment then—for Humbert Humbert and for us, once we know the story of his growing up and his frustrated search for happiness—when the would-be lodger steps onto Charlotte Haze's "piazza" and sees his "Riviera love" peering at him. It is the dunk-and-taste of the *petite madeleine,* all time and distance collapsing in an instant's ecstatic conflagration, but with the difference that it is not the past that Humbert Humbert will return to, but the ceaseless prosecution of his re-inflamed desire.

Still, that desire, in all of its elegantly expressed carnality, has about it enough of the metaphysical quest for lost time to exert a definite mitigating effect. Somehow the sexual gets strangely conflated with the quixotic quest for a landing place outside of the endless succession of hours and days. Indeed, Humbert Humbert early on reflects on "the fey grace, the elusive, shifty, soul-shattering, insidious charm that separates the nymphet from such coevals of hers as are incomparably more dependant on the spatial world of synchronous phenomena than on that intangible island of entranced time where Lolita plays with her likes." Profane as is its outward physical expression, Humbert Humbert's deeper desire points him toward an Eliotic lost world where memory and desire are forever mixed.

But before I get too indulgent, too soft toward poor Humbert Humbert, I make myself remember that he is, charm and articulateness notwithstanding, a self-confessed child molester and murderer. Moreover, part of the whole experience of reading the novel is a wrestling with these periodic self-corrections, the inward swings from an empathic immersion to a posture of enflamed moral righteousness. Trying to draw a bead on Humbert Humbert, I'm forced to realize just how provisional all such moral bookkeeping must necessarily be.

The fascinating paradox about this pull toward Humbert Humbert is that, in many ways, it is an attraction "in spite of." And I don't just mean the obvious matter of his pedophilia. There is also his snobbism, his unrelenting cultural *hauteur*, the attitude that his own mind puts him above everyone he encounters, be it a hotel-desk clerk, a camp directress, or the formidably middlebrow Charlotte Haze. Most of us are coached from earliest childhood on to suspect and mock the snob and to unmask elitism as aggression and overcompensation. How is it that we fall in so readily with Humbert Humbert, delighting to see his high-culture fastidiousness collide with the ubiquitous manifestations of low-brow Americana? Nabokov's drollery is never more dead-on than when he inventories the features of the pop culture Lolita herself feasts upon:

> Sweet hot jazz, square dancing, goocy fudge sundaes, musicals, movie magazines and so forth—these were the obvious items in her list of beloved things. The Lord knows how many nickels I fed to the gorgeous music boxes that came with every meal we had! I still hear the nasal voices of those invisibles serenading her, people with names like Sammy and Jo and Eddy and Tony and Peggy and Guy and Patty and Rex, and sentimental song hits, all of them as similar to my ear as her various candies were to my palate. She believed, with a kind of celestial trust, any advertisement or advice

that appeared in *Movie Love* or *Screen Land*—Starasil Starves
Pimples, or "You better watch out if you're wearing your shirttails
outside your jeans, gals, because Jill says you shouldn't."

Humor has a way of distributing the loyalties. To laugh at something
is to side with the mocker, though the reader might also be feeling the tug
of the betrayer's conscience. With Humbert-the-humorous I find myself
siding against not only a gallery of individuals and types (mainly types—
the highlighting of typicality being one of Nabokov's most reliably witty
moves), but also the whole right-thinking, consumerist, boosterish ethos
of the American 1950s. Nothing is too small or trivial to escape Humbert
Humbert's caustic vigilance, not even the manner in which the mistress
of Lolita's summer camp refunds his money when he comes to withdraw
his "daughter" early: ". . . hag Holmes writing out a receipt, scratching her
head, pulling a drawer out of her desk, pouring change into my impatient
palm, then neatly spreading a banknote over it with a bright '. . . and five!';
photographs of girl-children; some gaudy moth or butterfly, still alive,
safely pinned to the wall. . . ." The passage is amusing, to be sure—the
pace, the precision, the way I can't but feel the anticipatory anxiety just
behind Humbert Humbert's hypervigilance—but the effect is to enlist me,
the reader, in his cause, to have me pulling for him as the embattled last
man of sensibility in a culture gone Yahoo.

Humbert Humbert's fastidiousness, combined with his distaste for
the manners and mores of his adopted country, generates a good deal of
the novel's humor—the humor of a refined sensibility excruciatingly at
odds with its world. But it creates as well the implicit situational comedy of the work—this intensely critical and worldly man, this European
gentleman, is utterly enslaved by his longing for a raucous, gum-cracking
thirteen-year-old. What could be less outwardly plausible, really? But the
fact that I am persuaded, drawn into this land of unlikeliness, makes the
investment all the greater and the eventual emotional payoff all the more
powerful.

Humbert Humbert and Lolita together propose a highly complex psychological dynamic. From the first, so Nabokov makes it seem, we find

an even match. Humbert Humbert has age, power, sophistication, and a playbook of subtle wiles. What Lolita has, equal to all of this, is her recognition of his desire and need and an instinctual awareness that all of his impressive attributes count for little when the point is to compel affection. Lolita plays expertly upon Humbert Humbert's desire, and his awareness of his corrupt criminality, extorting favors, charging fees for services rendered, and keeping her captor perpetually uncertain, ultimately inducing in him the paranoia that makes the fantastical presence of Clare Quilty possible.

Lolita's own culpability, her collusion, is a key issue in any interpretation of Humbert Humbert's guilt. It certainly was for my class. We returned to this one matter over and over, especially after viewing Lyne's film, which casts the girl described as "four foot ten in one sock" as a pouty vixen with very nearly a woman's body. It was the misrepresentation my students took issue with, as much as Lyne's suggestion that Lolita may have taken pleasure in Humbert Humbert's assaults. But the novel, too, is full of ambiguities. Humbert Humbert makes much of the fact that when he finally has sex with Lolita on their first morning at *The Enchanted Hunters,* she is not even a virgin, having been (she tells him) initiated just recently by the camp mistress's son. And his aim is transparently self-exonerating when he addresses the "Frigid gentlewomen of the jury," and confides: "I am going to tell you something very strange: it was she who seduced me."

Humbert Humbert acts as if Lolita's expressed desire has suddenly leveled the playing field. How guilty is the poor man who is, in point of fact, seduced by an avid young girl who is not even a virgin? But Humbert Humbert's protestations ring hollow. He does not really expect the reader to be swayed in his judgment. The information is offered by Nabokov more to fill out the psychological portraiture than to ease our sense of his culpability. The memoir is written by a man well aware of his guilt, and our recognition of this helps explain our troubled sympathy for him.

Such is Nabokov's devious strategy, however, that the reader never comes to rest in a morally unambiguous place. But this is not because our author is evading the responsibility of closure. Rather, he is offering the difficult truth that while we may cherish moral absolutes philosophically and use them to help guide our behavior, they do not exist situationally. Nabokov may have rejected the hydraulic push-pull gestalt of Freud's analysis, but the two shared a kindred view of psychic complexity and of the impetuous—overruling—force of needs and desires. Where these are in active play, the moralist must despair of certainties.

For this reason, *Lolita* functions as a kind of moral growth chart. Younger readers, like my Mt. Holyoke students, and like me in my early twenties, are more shocked—or titillated—by Humbert Humbert's lusts and scheming transgressions, and the main tension seems to be between the depravity of the imagining and the beauty of the language that portrays it. Certainly much of our classroom conversation centered on this. My sense is that the focus would shift decisively if we were to reconvene ten years later for another reading—or am I just universalizing my own shift of awareness? When I read the novel most recently it was the flawed, heartbreaking, *tragic* Humbert Humbert who stood before me, and his situation seemed more pathetic and less morally deplorable. The second half of the book makes this understanding increasingly clear: it is possible to start feeling for the man, and in the process become aware of yourself growing as a reader.

If Humbert Humbert initially has the upper hand (Lolita has not been told that her mother has died), this changes by degrees as the narrative progresses, as his guilt betrays him into a growing paranoia and as Lolita, grasping his uneasiness, begins playing the cat-and-mouse games that will end in her escape and the collapse of his world. For instance, not only does she change the letters and numbers of their pursuer's license plate (noted at Humbert Humbert's request), but she also leaves the telltale smudge—why else but to make him frantic with suspicion?

The psychological—and, it turns out, literal—agent of Humbert Humbert's dissolution is the playwright Quilty, the shifty "Cue" who slips so maddeningly in and out of view through the second half of the novel. Bit player in terms of his actual text appearances, Quilty is the most intriguing of figures. He is at once figment and fact, shadow and substance; he is all innuendo and supposition. While his existence *is* established and corroborated over the course of the novel, Nabokov delights in playing an elaborate shell game with his persona.

The earliest reference to Quilty, so oblique as to slip right by the first-time reader, is in the third paragraph of John Ray Jr.'s peculiar Forward, where he remarks with brisk casualness on the fates of many of the novel's characters, his mention of Mrs. Richard F. Schiller's (Lolita's) death in childbirth vying with Virginia Woolf's sentence-long revelation of Mrs. Ramsay's death in *To the Lighthouse,* for uninflected brevity.

It is here, too, that the reader learns that the ever-so-shadowy Vivian Darkbloom, ostensibly a collaborator of Quilty's, "has written a biography called 'My Cue,'" rumored to be her best work. "Cue," Humbert Humbert later announces, is one of Quilty's nicknames. Then, some pages later, as Humbert Humbert takes up residence in the Haze house, news comes that one Ivor Quilty, a relation of the playwright, is a neighbor, and later still, when there is discussion of lewd behaviors noted at local Hourglass Lake, Charlotte's friend Jean mentions Ivor, adding, suggestively, before the arrival of her husband cuts her short: "Last time he told me a completely indecent story about his nephew. It appears—" I am not about to chart Quilty sightings here, only suggesting that Nabokov's deliberately tantalizing treatment of the man leaves the door open to imaginings, encouraging his readers to fall in more readily with Humbert Humbert's escalating paranoia about the quicksilver figure he is convinced is following him and Lolita across the country.

That adjective—"quicksilver"—does double-duty here, not only characterizing the fluid slipperiness of Quilty's presence in the novel, but also hinting at mirrors and at the role he comes to play as Humbert Humbert's quasi alter ego.

Nabokov loves nothing better than games, puzzles, symmetries, reversals, encoded allusions—any and all of the artifices whereby the chaotic momentum of life can be given pattern and be served up as a self-contained system of meaning. It makes great sense that Humbert Humbert should have a double—the perfect duplication of name and surname has already planted the subliminal suggestion—but we should be careful not to push too hard at the mapping of correlations. Quilty is a sketchy—penumbral—alter ego at best. Although he is, as Humbert Humbert at one point observes, a "fellow of my age," he is flashier in his manner and, as we later learn, far more licentious in his practices. What he shares with the narrator is an obsession with nymphets and a cultivated sensibility that is skewed toward codes and elaborate wordplay. This latter fixation figures importantly once Lolita has disappeared and Humbert Humbert tracks her spoor through the encrypted jokey references Quilty leaves in various hotel and motel registers (e.g., "Harold Haze, Tombstone, Arizona").

Throughout the novel, Humbert Humbert and Quilty are held together in the gravitational field of their fixation on Lolita. This paradoxical bonding finds its playful—and hilarious—outer expression in their first interchange at *The Enchanted Hunters.* Humbert Humbert, waiting for the sleeping pills he has given Lolita to take effect, stands on the porch in the dark. He hears someone drinking from a screw-top bottle, and then a voice:

> "Where the devil did you get her?"
> "I beg your pardon?"
> "I said: the weather is getting better."
> "Seems so."
> "Who's the lassie?"
> "My daughter."
> "You lie—she's not."
> "I beg your pardon?"
> "I said: July was hot. Where's her mother?"
> "Dead."

The beautiful byplay of misheard and actual, insinuation and bedeviled conscience, pulls the two men into a strange accord and signals the eventual joining of their fates. Nabokov delights in the possibilities offered by their "relationship." When he writes that final scene, for example, of Humbert Humbert confronting Quilty with his sins (which are, of course, his own sins), he cleverly turns the situation inside out: if before Humbert Humbert could not make out the stranger speaking to him in the dark, now it is Quilty who does not recognize his stalker.

QUILTY SHARES Humbert Humbert's obsession with Lolita's nymphet beauty, which is strong enough to compel elaborate subterfuges and epical cross-country travels. Stealing her away, he has dealt Humbert Humbert the ultimate narcissistic injury, and for this he must die. Indeed, the desire for revenge very nearly trumps all other fixations as Humbert Humbert finally comes face to face with Lolita—now a very pregnant Mrs. Richard F. Schiller—after years of frustrated searching. As soon as he learns from her that it was Quilty who was the agent of his ruin, he can scarcely contain his murderous fury. The fact that Lolita, whom he credited with her own sexual volition from the start, should have been a party to the deed does not seem to distress him as much as we suppose it might. His rage is pointed directly at his adversary. After extending a last halfhearted and obviously futile invitation to Lolita—that she leave with him then and there—he drives away. The reader feels how his focus has shifted. Within pages he has run Quilty to ground in his disheveled manse, and in a scene of graphically surreal intensity he has finished him off with his pistol: "I hit him at very close range through the blankets, and then he lay back, and a big pink bubble with juvenile connotations formed on his lips, grew to the size of a toy balloon, and vanished."

Nabokov has written a lurid and overblown climactic scene, and I have never taken it seriously. It is, along with the *deus ex machina* death of Charlotte Haze, part of the other, artifice-laden *Lolita,* and has curiously little to do with my response to the novel, which is about love and the remorseless work of time. That Lolita is a mere girl, a nymphet, makes Humbert Humbert's obsession scandalous, no question—it sets a whole dramatic machinery into motion. But somehow this is not the novel's true center of gravity, which lies deeper and carries a more universal thrust. For me the power of *Lolita* is found in the peculiar focus of erotic will that allows Humbert Humbert to feel with exquisite sensitivity the shocks of time. His mania has become a kind of magnifying device. The pathos is terrible. Whatever blow any of us would feel setting eyes upon a former lover changed by the passage of years, is for him intensified. His luscious girl-child has become a woman. Worn and blowsy, *pregnant,* she is once and for all outside the enchanted realm of his projections. And insofar as Humbert Humbert's nymphet fixation has been, at some level, a desperate search for a connection outside what he earlier called "the spatial world of synchronous phenomena," he has not only lost his original

Lolita forever—to Quilty, to Schiller, to the years—but I feel he has lost the dream of time regained as well. For Humbert Humbert, who has invested himself entirely in his mania, there is nothing left.

Except—and this is the double recognition that transfigures everything and lifts the novel from fascination to greatness—except that Humbert Humbert understands both the nature of his guilt and the sad, wrenching truth that becomes his partial redemption. In the wake of a sequence of slowly surfacing memories—detonations of the past—he is made to realize and suffer the knowledge that he robbed from Lolita the core of her childhood and what family love she had, admitting that "even the most miserable of family lives was better than the parody of incest, which, in the long run, was the best I could offer the waif."

Humbert Humbert's most heartbreaking recognition comes just paragraphs from the end. In flight from the scene of the crime at Quilty's mansion, he has an unexpected flash, recalling how, just days after Lolita first disappeared, a sudden wave of nausea had caused him to stop his car at a roadside. There, on the outskirts of a small mining town, he hears a "vapory vibration of accumulated sounds"—children playing. And in that mingling of distant voices he realizes—it is the half-sentence that changes everything for the reader—that "the hopelessly poignant thing was not Lolita's absence from my side, but the absence of her voice from that concord." Just this, nothing more, but it marks Humbert Humbert's stunning and sudden protrusion into humanity.

Now—at last—when his love has fully emerged, the scenes we have witnessed can deliver their accumulated weight. Now I fully believe his earlier assertion, when he faces Lolita as she is, grown and stripped of every remnant of her original provocative appeal, that he loves her absolutely, beyond contingency. "You may jeer at me," writes Humbert Humbert, "and threaten to clear the court, but until I am gagged and half-throttled, I will shout my poor truth. I insist the world know how much I loved my Lolita, *this* Lolita, pale and polluted, and big with another's child, but still gray-eyed, still sooty-lashed, still auburn and almond, still Carmencita, still mine. . . ."

There it is—all at once the corruption, and our judgment of the corruption, has been transformed. Humbert Humbert has burst the dreary limit of his shell. He has turned inside-out from being the possessor, the taker, to being the bestower. How perfectly ironic—and just—that Lolita grasps none of it. In their final scene together, she faces down Humbert Humbert's terrible need and sorrow and turns down his request to come away with him with the casual assertion: "I would sooner go back to Cue."

At the every end—a spurned lover, a jailed killer, a man who has lost the all-consuming dream of repossessing the past—Humbert Humbert seizes his final recourse. He redirects the course of his love from its original specific—transitive—desire for Lolita to the intransitive celebration of making, writing. The murderer with his fancy prose style has discovered "the refuge of art," adding, to close out his confession, "And this is the only immortality you and I may share, my Lolita."

I am devastated every time I read these words. I feel not only the distance I've traveled from my slightly prurient engagement in the early chapters—it's hard not to feel, guiltily or not, the erotic pulse of Humbert Humbert's obsession—to the tragic collapse of a tormented elderly man. But there is little sense of triumph, little cackling over just deserts, for between beginning and end we've seen lust somehow grow into love. I don't know if it's possible to read about the immolation of another's loss without drawing on our own experience in those realms.

HER NAME IS the first word and the last, and the story of Humbert Humbert's tortured devotion takes up everything in between. The structure is circular and in this way reinforces the subliminal sense of love beyond change. Is this enough to redeem the pedophilia? Not for the moral guardians who originally banned the novel. But for my students, yes. I had thought that they would bridle at the premise as well as the high artifice. I saw that I had, not for the first time, underestimated the deeper swaying powers of art. Their response showed me a great deal. Figuratively speaking, there was not a dry eye in the house.

The Possibility of the Search

Walker Percy's *The Moviegoer*

H ERE IT IS, the joy and mystery of reading, the whole matter synop-
sized for me in this one little ceremony of private renewal, all be
ginning with the extraction from under pounds of piled-up other books
of the slim blue Avon paperback of Walker Percy's *The Moviegoer*. I'd read
and re-read the novel some years ago, zooming in on it with a sense of
intimate possessiveness each time, but then, for who knows what reason,
I'd allowed it to subside back into latency. I hadn't much thought of it
for years (the way you can live without even a thought of some person
who was once at the very center of your existence), the business of other
books shouldering it aside—or maybe it was just that the last encounter
had temporarily done its work, placating or discharging whatever obscure
needs are at the heart of the secret Masonic life of reading.

The Moviegoer is a quiet novel and for that reason maybe easy to forget
about, though under its placid surface run some strong currents. It gives
account of a period of time around Mardi Gras in the life of Binx Bolling.
Binx is a young man living in New Orleans; he is in some deep—and to
me utterly familiar—way lost to himself. Turning as it does on his reaction to a spiritual crisis in the life of his second cousin, Kate, whom he
loves, *The Moviegoer* has been read as a work of religious exploration. But
I am not religious, and I have never read it for these messages. For me,
Percy's novel is very much about the self in limbo, poised between the
suspicion of meaning and the simultaneous fear that meaning may finally

be nothing more than a face-saving construct, a bridge between one day and the next, a frail invention holding at bay the harsher truth of things, that Burroughsian vision of the naked lunch—reality—quivering raw at the tip of the fork. And if Binx does feel the balance finally—hesitantly—tip toward meaning, in his case toward God, I can no longer recall if I ever seconded him on his, or any, terms. To be honest, when I recently returned to *The Moviegoer,* I didn't even remember quite how things had finally played out. That was not the draw—or the point—of the book for me. What had stayed behind, preserved vividly—even if I had not seen fit to tap it for the longest time—was the idea and the feeling of what Binx called the "search."

This notion was, and remains, one of my few readerly touchstones, which I don't mean in the Matthew Arnold sense of being an excellence I use to measure other excellences by, but rather in the sense of being one of my interior coordinates. If I were able to do the impossible—to draw the map of my inwardness, the *terra incognita* of my thought and dream world, my fundamental self—then Percy's articulation of the "search" would be there as a distinctive topographical reference point, along with Charles Swann's jealousy, Emma Bovary's fickle romantic frenzy, Humbert Humbert's criminal fastidiousness, Mrs. Ramsay's buzzing inner life, and a number of other essential expressions. Like these, Binx's search has become one of those literary imaginings that feels more real on the page than does its actual counterpart version in my own life, because even as it draws on my deepest identifications it also exceeds them.

The "search." The mention of it comes early in the novel, sudden and electric, and I could not, before, nor can I now, read it without feeling everything inside me shift, supposedly important things becoming instantly incidental, a sense of alerted expectation radiating directly into my life, at that moment altering entirely my sense of the world. First, though, I have to make clear how mired Binx is in the ordinariness of his office routines, his noncommittal relationships with his pretty secretaries, and his frequent visits to his aunt's house. "I am a model tenant and a model citizen," he affirms, "and take pleasure in doing all that is expected of me."

Binx is a man caught in the dread daily circuit, to the point where he cannot even imagine that life might hold change or open trapdoors under his feet. Fittingly, not surprisingly, I was myself in such a lockstep when I first picked the book up. In my early thirties, working, as I had been for long months, in a bookstore in Ann Arbor, Michigan, I was young enough to still believe that the great surprises and transformations were all still to come, but no longer so young as to assume that their coming was a matter of course. I would write, I would write great works, but when would I begin? When would the confirming flash light up my sky? And was the story of the great love already told, or was there more to come? I look back now and I see a young man living what the philosopher Søren Kierkegaard, one of Percy's tutelary spirits, categorized as the despair that is unaware of itself as being despair.

Binx is in the same situation, and once Percy has established just how deeply he is enslaved by habit he is free to shake things up. Here is the relevant passage:

> But things have suddenly changed. My peaceful existence in Gentilly has been complicated. This morning, for the first time in years, there occurred to me the possibility of a search. I dreamed of the war, no, not quite dreamed but woke with the taste of it in my mouth, the queasy-quince taste of 1951 and the Orient. I remembered the first time the search occurred to me. I came to myself under a chindolea bush. Everything is upside-down for me, as I shall explain later. What are generally considered to be the best times are for me the worst times, and that worst of times was one of the best. My shoulder didn't hurt but it was pressed hard against the ground as if somebody sat on me. Six inches from my nose a dung beetle was scratching around under the leaves. As I watched, there awoke in me an immense curiosity. I was onto something. I vowed that if I ever got out of this fix, I would pursue the search. Naturally, as soon as I recovered and got home, I forgot all about it. But this morning when I got up, I dressed as usual and began as usual to put my belongings into my pockets: wallet, notebook (for writing down occasional thoughts), pencil,

keys, handkerchief, pocket slide rule (for calculating percentage returns on principal). They looked both unfamiliar and at the same time full of clues. I stood in the center of the room and gazed at the little pile, sighting through a hole made by thumb and forefinger. What was unfamiliar about them was that I could see them. They might have belonged to someone else. A man can look at this little pile on his bureau for thirty years and never once see it. It is as invisible as his own hand. Once I saw it, however, the search became possible. I bathed, shaved, dressed carefully, and sat at my desk and poked through the little pile in search of a clue just as the detective on television pokes through the dead man's possessions, using his pencil as a poker.

My first impulse after quoting at such length is to apologize, as if I were in some violation of literary good manners. This would be the legacy of years put in on the reviewing treadmill—this along with the feeling that I had better get started doing my duty, troweling on the context, pouncing on salient features of the prose, adducing precedents, and then building the cud, that pulpy mass of thematic relevance that I can chew and digest in one of my four commodious stomachs.

But this time I resist all such impulses. I refuse to be bashful about asking for extra attention for a passage I have marked out as pivotal, nor do I feel the least call to follow the standard format for the reassessment of a favorite book. Caught up though I was once again in Percy's orchestration of a turning point in Binx's life, his recognitions en route to what he calls, after the poem by Dylan Thomas, his "thirtieth year to heaven," and struck as I was—repeatedly—by his occasions of lyricism, his bittersweet romance with New Orleans, its characters and atmospheres, I now feel the pull to something different. I want to think about the obscure ways in which a novel (and this one passage in particular) has insinuated itself into my life and what associations it generates outside the closed circle of the literary reading.

When I first read this section however many years ago, I felt one of the rare thrills of reading. I mean the sudden and complete puncturing of the screen of illusion, that slightly detached engagement we create by way of our customary suspension of disbelief. Until I reached that passage I was filtering the world through Binx's wryly agreeable and existentially astute persona, pilfering what I could to sharpen my own take on the poignant ironies of modern life, but essentially reading—turning pages while wrapped up in a uniquely charged elsewhere. When I arrived at the "search" passage, however, my engagement right away changed. It was as if I stepped through some transparent wall and into the book. As Binx described watching the beetle and awakening to "an immense curiosity," a sense of being "onto something," I felt a powerful kindred emotion. It was as if someone were tapping me on the shoulder. Binx's being onto the possibility of a search put me onto the same possibility. It was—and here the cliché suits the purpose—as if I had been waiting all my life for this little spark of validation. I was suddenly looking at my own experience with the same detached regard.

I have always had my own relation to the idea of the search, which, difficult as it is to characterize, is nevertheless an impulse as clear and per-suasive as that of love. It seems as if the more primary a feeling is, the less amenable it is to characterization. For me the word "search," used in the way Percy uses it, is code for a vast intuition that has haunted me for as long as I can remember. Founded in—or maybe causing—a sense of estrangement from the universally agreed upon business of living, this in-tuition proposes that daily active life is but a surface play; however com-plicated and intriguing it might be, it is not the real story. Indeed, that busy outer life *masks* the real story, distracts us from it. The feeling would ambush me without warning as far back as early childhood, when I would from time to time catch myself suddenly frozen in a family moment, star-ing out past the dishes on the table or the implements of some job I was supposed to be doing, convinced that it was all a kind of projection on a screen, just behind which—if I could only find a way to break through—something breathtakingly essential was to be found. My business, my task, I knew, was to use whatever means I'd been given to discover what was there. And fail as I have to reach anything remotely conclusive, I remain watchful. Curiously, though, I have always held what for others would be a religious feeling in a nonreligious way, resisting all practices and disciplines and narratives of faith. I ply my resistance, even as I recognize that any such notion of "a story" all but presupposes a teller.

For me the rest of the novel arranged itself around this moment. Binx had, in that earlier passage, tuned in not just to the mystery of life—that staple topic of my adolescent and adult ruminations—but he had framed with perfect intensity the *noir*ish thrill, the sense of dark consequence, that goes along with such a recognition. There remained only to turn the pages and study how the mystery played out. How would the next hundred sixty some pages do justice to this riveting announcement?

Well, they didn't, certainly not in the way I had hoped. After the midpoint of the novel the focus shifts away from Binx in his isolation. Following Percy's Kierkegaardian notions, the plot moves to the "ethical" plane, requiring relationship and complication. His aunt, worried about the well-being of her daughter, Kate, asks Binx to look after her, and as he gets involved in what feels to her like a life-or-death crisis of meaning, he finds his detached equanimity shattered. He grasps, if only at one remove—a "contact high"—the urgency of spiritual need, and he is nudged in the direction of change. By novel's end, Binx has had a searing exposure to the paradox-afflicted human heart, but he has gained on enlightenment only slightly. He has adjusted his metaphysics and come within range of faith. But if he has at last experienced the question, he has not yet found in himself any response commensurate with the urgency of the call.

From my reader's perspective—and this no doubt tells much about my own state—it almost doesn't matter, not so far. *The Moviegoer*, as it has entered my life, does not depend for its importance on the answers it gives. It has reached me with its asking and the agitations that asking has provoked in my life; this is how it perpetuates itself. Is this odd? I don't know. One might suppose this awareness, this wondering, is a condition more suited to adolescence, part of a bookish boy's Dostoevsky phase, and that long immersions in the banality of daily life would have rubbed the edge off the impulse.

But no, it would seem that certain books, certain writers, certain ideas have their own designs on us. *The Moviegoer* recently resurfaced in my life in a way that makes me question—not for the first time—the workings of what some might dismissively shrug off as mere coincidence.

Maybe coincidence is not the best word. Coincidence refers to the simultaneous occurrence of two thematically related events, which often creates in the onlooker the suspicion that there may, in fact, be some patterning intelligence in the world. But my Walker Percy encounter feels like something else again; it has more to do with how we store and retrieve the important contents of our inner lives, and how those meanings—or awarenesses—then act upon us.

As I noted, though I was once a great reader of Walker Percy—his essays as well as his fiction—I hadn't given the work much thought in recent years. He had stopped writing—had died, in fact—and I had turned to other things. This might be another way of saying that I had let go of the idea of the search, or—the reverse—had flattered myself that it was now so much second nature that I didn't need the old trigger. But the fact that it struck me again with such clear force suggests that this was not the case.

My reconnection came quite suddenly last spring and was the result of one of those chains of chance that most readers will recognize. I was having my regular Monday lunch with my friend and teaching colleague out at Mt. Holyoke, when a turn in the conversation brought a mention of Percy. I forget the context, but I do remember very clearly how my friend and I let go of whatever we were on and followed the digression instead, reminding each other of what we knew but had somehow forgotten—we were both great fans of the writer and of *The Moviegoer* in particular. I love these sidebars, these abrupt shifts, for while they don't always add to the immediate discussion, they are confirmations, subtle reminders of the meeting of minds that makes discussion possible. In that pause we flashed from idea to sensibility, acknowledging as we did that each of us had stood in that other place, the unguarded private zone where Percy had reached us. And then we resumed, as before, but refreshed, closer in to what matters.

That day, or the very next, I came home to find in the mail a review copy of a book by Paul Elie, *The Life You Save May Be Your Own,* which I glanced at enough to see that it was a group biography of four Catholic writers and thinkers: Thomas Merton, Dorothy Day, Flannery O' Connor, and Walker Percy. I felt a happy twinge when I saw Percy's name, and I took a minute to study the photographs, lingering especially on several shots of the young Percy, but also struck powerfully by the beauty of the young Flannery O'Connor, before the ravages of lupus. But just then there were things that needed doing, and the book was set aside.

Somehow, though, the slumbering thing had been wakened—Percy had worked his way back into my thoughts—and if anything argues for the mysterious purposefulness of the unconscious mind, it's the fact that a few days later, with no ulterior plan in mind, I found myself impulsively, but also decisively setting aside the whole afternoon to read through the Walker Percy sections of Elie's book. Doing this was enough to bring back the feeling of my old immersions, and the very same night I was rooting high and low through the chaos of my books, desperate to get my hands on my copy of *The Moviegoer*. Of course I couldn't, not right away. Had I lost it, loaned it? It was unthinkable to me, right then, in the middle of a weekday night, that I didn't have *The Moviegoer* somewhere among my books. I felt what might be called a "reader's panic," which is not so different, maybe, from the alarm that the drinker feels when he realizes that there is no more booze to be had. I debated driving the ten miles to the local Barnes & Noble. And very likely I would have, but just then I moved aside another stack and there it was, the object of my search, the most coveted item in the house, in the world, that bedraggled-looking little blue Avon paperback. I sat down right away to read the opening sentences, I reconnected instantly. I was back in Walker Percy's New Orleans; I had—at least such was the persuasive sensation—never been away. This was where I needed to be. I had forgotten, I had been remiss, but everything was fine now. And I knew that for the next day or so nothing would be quite as important as this private reconnaissance mission.

I was right. I fell promptly into the continuum of the book, experiencing as I did so the peculiar Kierkegaardian phenomenon of a "repetition," which Percy himself is so attuned to, and which Binx defines in somewhat gnarly prose as "the re-enactment of past experience toward the end of isolating the time segment which has lapsed in order that it, the lapsed time, can be savored of itself and without the usual adultera-tion of events that clog time like peanuts in brittle." He clarifies this with his example of his accidental re-encounter with a magazine ad, "show-ing a woman with a grainy face turned up to the sun." Says Binx: "Then I remembered that twenty years ago I saw the same advertisement in a magazine on my father's desk, the same woman, the same grainy face, the same Nivea Creme. The events of the intervening twenty years were neutralized, the thirty million deaths, the countless torturings, uprootings and wanderings to and fro. Nothing of consequence could have happened because Nivea Creme was exactly as it was before. There remained only time itself, like a yard of smooth peanut brittle."

I agree with Kierkegaard, Percy—and countless others—that this is one of the great mysteries, how we can on rare occasions short-circuit the relentless forward flow of time and connect ourselves, in a kind of psychic dissolve, to ourselves as we were. This is the illusion, anyway, for of course it's also true that the same words are necessarily filtered through a sensi-bility changed in a thousand ways by one's life experiences since the time of last exposure. Who had I been, then, fifteen or so years ago, re-reading this novel, and who was I now? Then—statistically a man in his middle thirties, already older than Binx, but still very much a boy living with the sense that the events and initiatives of his life were all yet before him. Now I am in many ways identifiably the same boy, but something has also changed. Without crisis or ceremony, without any announcement at all, a shift has taken place. The events and initiatives that were all in the future—the subjunctive—tense, have slipped by and become the deposit of the past. I was the same subjective self, but entirely different—what a strange zone I inhabited.

Percy was invading me, no question, though it was not at all clear to what end. Was it just that I needed this unexpected exposure, this en-counter, with an earlier—no doubt more intense—version of myself? Was I inviting the search back into my life? Had it ever really disappeared? Or was it time for a more sustained self-accounting? This invasion, or in-filtration, which does not happen to me with most of the reading I do, gave that strange *déjà vu* condition an added inflection. I felt not just the

ghostly superimposition of selves, but also the obscure thrill of the dou-
bled, or folded-over, awareness. By which I mean the very real sense that
just behind the performance of the day to day—conferencing with my
Mt. Holyoke undergrads, sitting in year-end meetings, driving to and fro
on the Mass Pike—a far more compelling scenario was unfolding, that of
the novel. And indeed, that scenario had such a pressing claim on me that
I felt that if I could only, somehow, lower the wattage of my immediate
surroundings, it would be revealed in its full vividness. I would discover
the story I was really wrapped up in while I was supposed to be living—
the one advertised through all those intimations. I write "supposed to
be living," and that "supposed" implies a kind of judgment, whereas the
greatest works of imagination make the case that real life is often elsewhere, and in this way they themselves judge us.

But why this book now? Was it a signpost in the strange land of midlife?
A goad, an incitement, a reminder, a reproach, a warning, an invitation?
Answering this would seem to be the purpose of the piece, its basic reason
for being. But having come to this point, where the deep logic of conception should take over, I find myself balking. For there followed no clear-cut
revelation, no sudden clarification. The process did not appear to lead me to
some necessary insight or make a change in my way of thinking about the
world—nothing so obvious. This is not a failure, nor even necessarily a narrative anticlimax. I don't think that reading has ever worked that way for me.
When I am not taking on a book for ulterior purposes—reviewing being the
most obvious—I don't ever really go to it for answers or thematic meanings
in any conventional sense. Rather, a novel for me is a pretext, a way of starting up and sustaining a complicated and many-layered inner exchange, a to-
and-fro which I long ago discovered that I need in order to locate myself in
the world. Reading is a process that keeps the inner realm open, susceptible.
Involvement in a book sets things going at a depth. If I cannot sink into
some virtual "other" place or triangulate my experience with that of another,
I feel that my life is lacking the shadows and overtones and the illusion of
added dimension that imagination provides. It feels flat to me.

I accept this as a peculiarity, a warp in my nature, and I often wonder
about its origins. I have accepted the terms. I understand that not every
novel—not even every "serious" novel—can do it for me. I have to hear

what I identify as the note of truth or tune in to an awareness that connects with my deepest sense of things. I need something like what I get
when Binx says, "What are generally considered to be the best times are
for me the worst times. . . ." When I read a sentence like this I have the
suddenly activated sense that my core solitude has been breached.

The search, then, was what I remembered and what brought me back
to the novel. I had, I'll admit it now, let myself grow away from that most
basic inner orientation and reading Percy put it back into my life. Not as
a permanent awareness, alas, but with the effect of a torch suddenly thrust
into a dark cave. The search. The idea of one's life as an urgent quest—as
a mystery calling for solution.

The reading was a reawakening, and who knows what effects it might
eventually produce. But no one can sustain an ongoing sense of awakening. An awakening is a shift, a jolt, not an ongoing condition. Already,
truth be told, the urgency has started to succumb to the tide of habit.
Hard as it is to see the purest thing, it's harder still to hold it intact, to
keep the flame from going out. My only immediate consolation is that
I have found, quite serendipitously, a way of marking it—underlining it in
memory to keep it near.

In this recent reading of *The Moviegoer* there was one moment—a moment outside the book—that imprinted the whole event for me. Already
it's the best memory, maybe the point of it all. It happened on a late April
afternoon. I was in South Hadley, done with the day's teaching, waiting
to go to a year-end picnic. I was sitting in my car, parked under a big tree
that had begun to shed its blossoms. The window was open, the world
felt like spring, and I was reading a scene in the novel where Binx goes to
visit his mother at the fishing camp where she lives with her stepfather. I
noticed only peripherally that the dark clouds were moving in and that
the wind was picking up. I got to the passage where Binx, who has been
sleeping on a screened porch, wakes up in the early dawn and watches his
mother go down to the dock with a casting rod and a wax-paper bundle:

Mother undoes the bundle, takes out a scout knife and pries loose
the frozen shrimp. She chops off neat pink cubes, slides them
along the rail with her blade, stopping now and then to jiggle her

nose and clear her throat with the old music. To make sure of
having room, she goes out to the end of the dock, lays back her
arm to measure, and casts in a big looping straight-arm swing, a
clumsy yet practiced movement that ends with her wrist bent in,
in a womanish angle. The reel sings and the lead sails far and wide
with its gyrating shrimp and lands with hardly a splash in the light
etherish water. Mother holds still for a second, listening intently
as if she meant to learn what the fishes thought of it, and reels in
slowly, twitching the rod from time to time.

A moment later he adds: "I pull on my pants and walk out barefoot
on the dock. The sun has cleared the savannah but it is still a cool milky
world. Only the silvery wood is warm and raspy underfoot." Two worlds,
just like that. I look up when the first splashing drops hit the windshield
and the wind lifts that original cool freshness off the grass. It comes to me
that Percy is about to launch forth on a bit of religious reflection, but at
this moment I am as far from that kind of thinking as can be and I pause.
I hold the mood of the afternoon, the mood of the passage. They vibrate
together, bleed into each other. And then for just an instant something
about the light around me, that "silvery wood," and the way I am perched
between here and there, containing both, cuts me free. I feel that I have
arrived at the brink. I am at the very place where the search might begin.

The Saddest Story, Indeed

Ford Madox Ford's *The Good Soldier*

MENTION FORD MADOX FORD'S *The Good Soldier* to anyone who knows the novel and it's very likely that you will get the first sentence quoted, or misquoted, back to you. "This is the saddest story I have ever heard." Like "Call me Ishmael" or Jane Austen's "It is a truth universally acknowledged . . . ," Ford's opener is more than a place to begin; it is a certificate of absolute rightness, like a name that sticks and in sticking somehow takes on the essential nature of the thing in question. *The Good Soldier,* for me at least, *is* the saddest of novels, and I found that when I went back to it a few months ago I was again entirely susceptible to its spell, its vision of love—or whatever it is that disfigures the lives of these characters—as a kind of sickness unto death. This time the sadness made it hard to get through the later parts of the book—it seemed to connect with so much I was at some level going through. Ford is so remorseless in his depictions, and so persuasive in his rhythmic forward thrust, that to turn the pages is almost to accede to a vision of absolute hopelessness. I did push on, of course, but it was with a dark, churning fascination, trying to recall, all these years since I first read it, whether there was finally any redemption offered for all the suffering. There wasn't, and it's this fact, more than what happens between the characters, that retroactively gives that opening sentence its ring of absolute rightness.

Writing these words, looking for a way in, I'll admit that I registered a pang of doubt, the sense of a shadow falling down to one side of my certainty. In some cases this would be enough to make me strike the beginning and look for a new point of entry. But here I held off because with that hesitation came an inkling that I might have also located a point of friction, a way of getting my hooks into a novel that in its plot and narration offers up what might be called a perfect "no stick" surface. For if there is any received wisdom, any "book," on *The Good Soldier,* it's that the narrator, Dowell, is the classic unreliable voice. Dowell so consistently alters and revises his presentation of events and his attribution of motives that the critic has a very hard time making any approach that does not in some obvious way question the uses of veracity.

The thing that struck me as I sat musing on that word "saddest"—and then the idea of sadness itself—was that it was applicable to the novel, but only at one remove. If we are strict about definitions then there is nothing essentially *sad* about the relations between the four principal characters— Dowell, his wife, Florence, and their great friends the Ashburnhams, Edward and Leonora—for sadness is a binding emotion, a feeling of loss that nonetheless signals the reality of a connection, present or former. But if the reader takes away any one recognition from Ford's novel, it is that these human relationships have been governed from the first by deceit, illusion, and whipped-up yearnings that have little or nothing to do with the flow of genuine affection between people. Behind the masks, the pretenses, the egotistical negotiations, blows an icy wind. Not one of the characters can be said to love another—not if we go by their actions. The novel is a terrifying presentation of loveless circumstances, a torturous peeling away of sustaining appearances. Desolation, yes—but sadness?

The Good Soldier is subtitled *A Tale of Passion,* and here, too, I pause. What exactly *is* passion, and how does it drive the novel forward? Can passion coexist with other kinds of love, or is it exclusive? Can passion divorced from love result in anything but tragedy? Tolstoy and Flaubert would probably agree that it cannot. Both in their great novels of adultery played off a primary split between the irrational uprooting force of passion (what Anna felt for Vronsky, Emma for Rodolphe) and the homing pull that is domestic love (at least on the part of Karenin and Charles). They would see passion as a sensuous imperative, bound to the lust that seeks to quench itself in another, more a push for release and self-extinction than the sustainable mutuality that is psychologically essential to the making of a family. Fittingly, there are no children in Ford's novel, none at all; among the couples there is nothing that resembles mutuality.

The opening pages of *The Good Soldier* are among the most seductive in all modern literature. Lyrical and dynamic, they are held aloft by the almost playful retrospective brio of Dowell's voice; it is as if, asserted sadness notwithstanding, he cannot resist revisiting in memory the beginning of things, the time before the fall. "We had known the Ashburnhams," he tells us in the second sentence, "for nine seasons of the town of Nauheim with an extreme intimacy—or, rather, with an acquaintanceship as loose and easy and yet as close as a good glove's with your hand." And, just a few pages on:

> Supposing that you should come upon us sitting together at
> one of the little tables in front of the club house, let us say, at
> Homburg, taking tea of an afternoon and watching the miniature
> golf, you would have said that, as human affairs go, we were an
> extraordinarily safe castle. We were, if you will, one of those tall
> ships with the white sails upon a blue sea, one of those things
> that seem the proudest and the safest of all the beautiful and safe
> things that God has permitted the mind of men to frame. Where
> better could one take refuge? Where better?

Drawn in, almost lulled by the beauty of the language, we are pulled up short when, right after, Dowell exclaims: "Permanence? Stability! I can't believe it's gone. I can't believe that that long, tranquil life, which was just stepping a minuet, vanished in four crashing days at the end of nine years and six weeks." And there you have it all, the insinuation of tragic outcome and the lively oscillation of this narrator's recounting of events, the spike-and-dip instability that establishes the ground of his notorious "unreliability." The passage creates in miniature the hyperbolic dynamic of reversal, of truths and secrets revealed, and gives a preview hint of the ararchic "passion" that eventually destroys the hand-in-glove intimacy of these two couples.

The Good Soldier is in many ways an infuriating novel to read, and of course this is Ford's intention. The narrating premise is that Dowell is telling the story of what happened to this group some time after the fact, performing a leisurely sort of postmortem, dispensing with strict sequence and patching in background history where it is needed. As he puts it: ". . . I shall just imagine myself for a fortnight or so at one side of the fireplace of a country cottage, with a sympathetic soul opposite me. And I shall go on talking, in a low voice while the sea sounds in the distance and overhead the great black flood of wind polishes the bright stars." But as the casual address is at every point at odds with the nature of the story he has to tell, the effect of his myriad foreshadowings and loaded asides is to build up an almost unbearable tension, with passages of willfully sustained illusion—the happy dream of appearances—repeatedly subverted by glimpses of the truth of things.

Ford's is a peculiar strategy. He has Dowell establish right at the outset that for most of the nine years of their friendship, he and Florence lived in perfect concord with the Ashburnhams. But at the very same time he is tearing down the illusion: "If for nine years I have possessed a goodly apple that is rotten at the core and discover its rottenness only in nine years and six months less four days, isn't it true to say that for nine years I possessed a goodly apple?" For all his insistence on the elegance and harmony of their "minuet," then, Dowell never lets us share in the blissful unknowing that he claims characterized his own experience. From the very start we are warned of the tragic outcome, and into every scene of his admittedly nonchronological telling he intrudes the insights yielded up by the forensics of hindsight. Yet he also keeps reminding us, scene after scene, of all that he did not know at the time. *The Good Soldier* does not set out to move us through any dramatization of lost illusions. It comes after us, rather, by way of its compulsions—Edward's toward helpless-seeming women, Leonora's toward the preservation of appearances, Florence's to conceal a past indiscretion, and Dowell's to locate, as it were, the black-box recorder that might explain once and for all what went wrong.

THE GIST OF THE STORY is roughly as follows. The Dowells and Ashburnhams befriend each other as sympathetic members of the leisured upper class at Nauheim, the spa they visit yearly, ostensibly because Florence and Edward each "have a heart." It is disclosed eventually (in Florence's case after her death) that neither has—or *had*—a medical condition. But the double-entendre sense of the phrase is operative throughout, though in complicatedly crosshatched ways. Florence is finally shown to have no heart at all—puncture her façade and you find nothing but clumps of cotton batting, whereas Edward—well, Edward is even more of a mystery.

For "nine seasons of the town of Nauheim" then, the couples meet, moving about in their orderly patterns, taking the waters, sightseeing, socializing over sumptuous meals, with nothing except Dowell's hindsight interpolations to ruffle the scene. But we soon discover that these interpolations *are* the story, and as they center mainly on Edward, he needs to be the focus.

Edward Ashburnham. To all appearances he is the perfectly evolved English gentleman. We catch sight of him first through Dowell's eyes as the narrator remembers sitting in the dining room of the spa, waiting for Florence:

> And then, one evening, in the twilight, I saw Edward Ashburnham lounge round the screen into the room. The head waiter, a man with a face all grey—in what subterranean nooks or corners do people cultivate those absolutely grey complexions?—went with the timorous patronage of those creatures towards him and held out a grey ear to be whispered into. It was generally a disagreeable ordeal for newcomers but Edward Ashburnham bore it like an Englishman and a gentleman. I could see his lips form a word of three syllables—remember I had nothing in the world to do but to notice these niceties—and immediately I knew he must be Edward Ashburnham, Captain, Fourteenth Hussars, of Branshaw House, Branshaw Teleragh.

Dowell, watching him, not only nails the nuances of manner and appearance, but in the process leaves no doubt at all as to his enthusiasm for the whole package:

> His face hitherto had, in the wonderful English fashion, expressed nothing whatever. Nothing. There was in it neither joy nor despair;

neither hope nor fear; neither boredom nor satisfaction. He seemed
to perceive no soul in that crowded room; he might have been
walking in a jungle. I never came across such a perfect expression
before and I never shall again. It was insolence and not insolence;
it was modesty and not modesty. His hair was fair, extraordinarily,
ordered in a wave, running from the left temple to the right; his
face was a light brick red, perfectly uniform in tint up to the roots
of the hair itself; his yellow moustache was as stiff as a toothbrush
and I verily believe that he had his black smoking jacket thickened
a little over the shoulder-blades so as to give himself the air of the
slightest possible stoop. It would be like him to do that; that was
the sort of thing he thought about. Martingales, Chiffney bits,
boots; where you got the best soap, the best brandy, the name of
the chap who rode a plater down the Khyber cliffs; the spreading power of number-three shot before a charge of number-four
powder. . . .

In this passage we see, as well, Ford's delightfully, maddeningly slip-
pery narrative technique, how the purity of Dowell's first impression, and
surmise, is gradually sifted through with information learned after the
fact. Given that Dowell makes increasing use of these hindsight perspectives as his narrative gets under way, this moment in the dining room is as
close as we get to finding out how Edward appeared from the outside, to
the appraising eyes of the world.

The split between appearances and underlying truths is the obvious
point of *The Good Soldier*. It is the ancient and inexhaustible theme—
societal codes versus the unsanctioned imperatives of need and desire.
Reading the novel as a younger man, I missed much of the implicit tension. I think I believed that we had all marched on, liberated ourselves
from hypocritical posturings—the social revolutions of our times had
done away with antiquated expectations of behavior. It took a few years of
adult exposure—to the academic world, to the cultures of child-rearing—
to grasp that the tyranny of appearances and assumed moralities is a human
constant and that only the codes of permission change over time.

Succinctly, Edward Ashburnham, for all his caste markings and schooling in "what is done," cannot resist the siren call of any pretty young woman who appears to need his care and protection. The whole reason he and Leonora first come to Nauheim, we find out, is to get away from a scandal Edward had caused by making an improper advance to a servant girl on a train in India. And who knows if she was the first? What we gradually discover over the course of Dowell's recounting of Edward's involvements is the truth of a loveless marriage. Loveless, at least, from Edward's side. Leonora, though Dowell insists she is passionate for her husband, is hard to see as anything but a woman tormented by the need to preserve appearances.

But the chronicling of Edward's indiscretions is hardly basis enough for a narrative. What ignites the deeper drama of the novel and brings the question of barren relationships to the fore is the spark that flies between Edward and Florence.

To talk about Edward and Florence—but also to fathom the underlying power of this novel—we need to acknowledge the extraordinary sexualized power of repression. This particular tension, directly bound to the religious and class-derived assumptions of time and place, may be foreign to the contemporary reader—I was myself a charter member of the Age of Aquarius—but the underlying power is readily tapped. We all understand the idea of the forbidden in our own way, and a novelist skilled at creating context and animating situation with gesture can make it vivid again. In Ford's world, strict societal prohibitions and rigid moral sanctions allowed the atmosphere to get so dense at key moments that the slightest movement could spark explosion. Indeed, one of the most powerful and implication-laden moments in the novel is, in terms of literal offense, as minimal as could possibly be.

Early on, in the first or second year of their "acquaintanceship" (Dowell himself is no longer sure), the two couples have gone, at Florence's urging, on a day-trip to visit a local castle. The trip is really an occasion for Florence to show off her learning, and she proceeds to lecture all who will listen on the historical importance of various features, a docent tour that culminates when she stops in front of a faded pencil draft of Martin Luther's protest.

Warming to her subject, she looks up at Edward and says, "'It's because of that piece of paper that you're honest, sober, industrious, provident, and clean-lived. If it weren't for that piece of paper you'd be like the Irish or the Italians or the Poles, but particularly the Irish. . . .'"

Then: ". . . she laid one finger upon Captain Ashburnham's wrist."

And there it is, the instigating, revealing moment. At a stroke, with a few sentences and the touch of a finger she has not only affronted Leonora—who we learn is Catholic and who takes her faith seriously enough to put divorce out of the question—but has also made it clear, at least as Dowell reconstructs the whole business, that she and Edward have an intimacy.

There is no easy way to make the tangle of things come clear—it could actually be that Dowell's associative rambling is the best course. The sequence of events tells us little, since the real dynamic of the novel has less to do with what happened than with Dowell's oddly pitched adumbration of connections and late-blooming realizations. Important here is that Edward and Florence were involved, and that Leonora found out and then sought to conceal the truth from Dowell. But more important is the fact that Edward, who just cannot seem to master his impulses, later "makes love" (which is to say pays affectionate attention) to Nancy, the young woman whom he and Leonora have taken into their care, and that Florence witnesses this and in her furious jealousy takes a fatal dose of capsules. In the wake of this, Edward, Leonora, and the girl return to England, where it is decided that Nancy should leave—the circumstance that proves to be the final blow. For it is upon receiving the telegram that Nancy has reached her destination that Edward goes out alone and cuts his throat.

A "tale of passion"? As Dowell says so often, in so many contexts, "I don't know." How do we ever fit the pieces together puzzle-style to make a picture? Too much is simply not clear—about the circumstances, but also about the English heart, which so far as Dowell, an American, is concerned, is beyond fathoming.

Re-reading *The Good Soldier* after some years, I found myself less interested than before in Dowell's status as an unreliable narrator. What does "unreliable" mean here anyway? That he is confused, self-conflicted, in denial, or just intentionally guileful? It could just be that he has forged for himself some uneasy compromise between the decorum of his class and the less savory "truth" that keeps trying to leak out. There is no one explanation. Maybe it's all of the above further combined with the inevitable partial and inaccurate nature of memory itself. But after several readings of the novel I find that I am less preoccupied with what really happened between these people—I have accepted that we are not meant to have the full picture—and more intent, vexed, by Edward's suicide.

This act is the gash at the heart of the novel and it leaves me unsettled and anxious. *The Good Soldier: A Tale of Passion.* I turn that subtitle over and over in my mind. But I just can't get the meaning to stick. When I think of other suicides—Emma Bovary's, Anna Karenina's—I see how passion, or its certain loss, offers the answer I need. But I can't understand Edward's decision in the same light. Unless there is more, much more, to be discovered in his relationship with Nancy, which seems similar enough to his other "affairs," passion is an unlikely cause. The more plausible explanation, I think, is that Nancy was just the figurative last straw; it was the failure of that connection to be a redemption that finally revealed to Edward the extremity of his situation, brought him face to face with the bankruptcy of his life. This interpretation accords, too, with Albert Camus' insight in *The Myth of Sisyphus,* his reflection on suicide—the act is not so much a violent impulse as the consummation of a gradual process, a steady undermining, which brings the person by degrees to the realization that his life is no longer tenable.

How, then, do we understand Edward? Certainly Dowell has never persuaded us that this is a man of passion in any usual sense. From the moment of first sighting in the dining room, through all of his vicissitudes, he has been presented as the very type of the repressed, inaccessible English gentleman, a gentleman governed in every social circumstance by his allegiance to the codes of his class. He is the "good soldier." And though as psychologizing sophisticates we will naturally theorize dammed-up reserves of unexpressed emotion—rage, lust—Ford is careful to curb that speculation, directing us instead, to a very different analysis.

There is a section almost midway in the novel where Dowell, trying to understand Edward's affairs, theorizes at some length about love and passion, desire and need, and this may be as close as the reader will come to understanding the deeper motivation of his suicide.

The background is the scene I mentioned earlier. Edward, in his role of guardian, has one night escorted Nancy, who is staying with them at Nauheim, to the casino. He ends up sitting on a bench in the park with her, and Florence, who has been tailing them, sees them together in the dark, to all appearances talking as lovers. Florence by this point is presumably no longer Edward's mistress. Still, overwhelmed by jealousy, she runs back to her rooms and takes her fatal dose of medicine.

Reconstructing all this, Dowell writes, apropos of Edward sitting in the park with Nancy: "He assured me—and I see no reason for disbelieving him—that until that moment he had had no idea whatever of caring for the girl. . . . Had he been conscious of it, he assured me, he would have fled from it as from a thing accursed. He realized that it was the last outrage upon Leonora. But the real point was his entire unconsciousness." Then, as Dowell recounts it, his familiar weakness overcame Edward, so that he ended up speaking of Nancy "as being the person he cared most for in the world," while Nancy, who admired him above all men, who saw him as the father she might have wished for, "naturally thought that he meant to except Leonora and she was just glad." Dowell tells us further: "It was like a father saying he approved of a marriageable daughter. . . . And Edward, when he realized what he was doing, curbed his tongue at once. She was just glad and went on being just glad."

"That," writes Dowell—and I honestly don't fathom what he means— "was the most monstrously wicked thing that Edward ever did in his life," though he next goes on to affirm in every way he can Edward's fundamental decency. But then—he is, after all, our tormenting narrator—he offers that: "Edward had no idea at all of corrupting her. I believe that he simply loved her. He said that that was the way of it and I, at least, believe him and I believe too that she was the only woman he ever really loved."

The reader has to register a shock here. A few minutes alone in the dark with a young woman and Edward has gone from having "no idea whatever of caring" for her to, at least in Dowell's mind, believing "that she was the only woman he ever really loved." And lest we conclude that Dowell has lost all purchase on the matter, he adds: "He said that that was so; and he did enough to prove it. And Leonora said that it was so and Leonora knew him to the bottom of his heart." One can only question what Dowell, or Leonora, or Edward—or, indeed, Nancy—understand by the word "love."

With this we come to what I believe is the real key passage in the novel, the two paragraphs in which Dowell presents a kind of philosophy of love as it might be applied to Edward. I quote them in full:

I have come to be very much of a cynic in these matters; I mean that it is impossible to believe in the permanence of man's or woman's love. Or, at any rate, it is impossible to believe in the permanence of any early passion. As I see it, at least, with regard to man, a love affair, a love for any definite woman, is something in the nature of a widening of the experience. With each new woman that a man is attracted to there appears to come a broadening of the outlook, or, if you like, an acquiring of new territory. A turn of the eyebrow, a tone of the voice, a queer characteristic gesture—all these things, and it is these things that cause to arise the passion of love—all these things are like so many objects on the horizon of the landscape that tempt a man to walk beyond the horizon, to explore. He wants to get, as it were, behind those eyebrows with the peculiar turn, as if he desired to see the world with the eyes that they overshadow. He wants to hear that voice applying itself to every possible proposition, to every possible topic; he wants to see those characteristic gestures against every possible background. Of the question of the sex instinct I know very little and I do not think that it counts for very much in a really great passion. It can be aroused by such nothings—by an untied shoelace, by a glance of the eye in passing—that I think it might be left out of the calculation. I don't mean to say that any great passion can exist without a desire for consummation. That seems to me a commonplace and to be therefore a matter needing no comment at all. It is a thing, with all its accidents, that must be taken for granted, as, in a novel, or a biography, you take it for granted that the characters have their meals with some regularity. But the real fierceness of desire, the real heat of a passion long continued and withering up the soul of a man, is the craving for identity with the woman that he loves. He desires to see with the same eyes, to touch with the same sense of touch, to hear with the same ears, to lose his identity, to be enveloped, to be supported. For, whatever may be said of the relation of the sexes, there is no man who loves a woman that does not desire to come to her for the renewal of his courage, for the cutting asunder of his difficulties. And that will be the mainspring of his desire for her. We are all so afraid, we are all so alone, we all so need from the outside the assurance of our own worthiness to exist.

So, for a time, if such a passion comes to fruition, the man will get what he wants. He will get the moral support, the encouragement, the relief from the sense of loneliness, the assurance of his own worth. But these things pass away; inevitably they pass away as the shadows pass across sun-dials. It is sad, but it is so. The pages of the book will have become familiar; the beautiful corner of the road will have been turned too many times. Well, this is the saddest story.

When I first read this passage, long before I thought to apply it to the case of Edward, I marked it for myself. Here, in a way that happens to me far too rarely, even with acknowledged works of "great literature," I felt addressed, if not explained to myself. I felt included in his "we," less alone in my own suspicions and recognitions, but at the same time chilled by the confirmation, the fact of it. Ford is not content to ground his reflection by simply pointing with a finger at love or desire, as if one or the other were somehow the transcendent origin of subjective value. Instead, he parts the curtain, asks what it is that underlies the pull, the impetus that impels men—heterosexual men, anyway—toward women. That he should demote, though hardly disavow, physical yearning, the "desire for consummation," strikes me as radical, and also true, though I can hardly pretend to speak for others. But reading Ford's explanation, it seemed right.

Physical desire was not the core, but the outer active expression, and what it expresses—beyond the maddening need for contact and release—is desire for a kind of merging that is less about taking the partner to oneself than about dissolving, awake and aware, into the other person. It is not about self-extinction, but rather about shedding the tormenting sense of final isolation, the loneliness that affects us most sharply right when the possibility of its relief is glimpsed. It is, as Ford puts it, about "the assurance of our own worthiness to exist," and that worthiness is only conferred through unconditional assent, the liquidation of boundaries.

The hard, controversial truth is that this romantic tension can't often be kept alive by one partner; for some men anyway, it tends to lose its charge, creating the terrible cycle of repetition, the Don Juan syndrome, which is the seducer's need to keep exchanging the object of his amorous attention. Since the charge is created by a kind of fantasy projection, once spent it cannot be re-created in the same person. The flaw is in the narcissism of the dreamer.

Don't we all deal with this in some way—the challenge of sustaining love, of keeping alive between ourselves and another the sense of energies in play? A relationship, a love, is not—in my experience anyway—a condition negotiated and then locked in like a mortgage rate. We not only need to *keep* feeling, but also to keep believing that we are actively met in the feelings of the other. I have yet to meet two humans who can generate the energy exchange without lapse. The long-term relationships I know, the ones that work, that prevail over time, have generous provisions for distance and diffusion; they are tolerant of what Marcel Proust called the "intermittencies of the heart." The essential thing is that the foundation of love be genuine—based in an original exchange of affections and deep feeling. Where this has not taken place, maybe because for psychological reasons it *could not* take place, the intensity has to be manufactured, projected onto the other. The fatal collapse of interest—which Ford attributes to a kind of expansion or growth in the lover—is more likely due to the fact that the fantasy impulse withers without variation; new idealizations depend on new stimulus scenarios, changed narratives.

The philosopher Søren Kierkegaard, who was such an influence on

Walker Percy, among others, is relevant here. His idea was that to break
the cycle, a person had to rise to another state of awareness, had to attain
the Ethical Stage, the second step of his three-part evolution (the third
being the Religious Stage). The Ethical Stage is the condition of constancy
symbolized by marriage, which I think is less about the mastery of desire
and more about getting over the idea that fulfillment is to be found seri-
ally, in other people. It is about dissolving the self-focus and accepting the
more embracing premise of mutuality. The biological point of marriage is,
of course, children. Edward and Leonora, like Dowell and Florence, are
childless. This is hardly just a novelistic convenience. Ford surely meant it
for a corroborating fact—idle and indolent, these people are dead-ended
in themselves, the end of their line.

Although *The Good Soldier* is subtitled *A Tale of Passion,* passion—at
least conventional passion—has very little to do with its tragic outcome.
Edward, our "good soldier," the incarnation of the highest attributes of his
social class, kills himself not out of an excess of pained desire for another,
but rather after confronting one last time the impossibility of ever finally
transcending his loneliness through love for another. Nancy's leaving is
not the cause of his decisive despair. She just happens to be the last in an
annihilating series. Edward might well have come to his tragic recognition
sooner; or he might have held it off indefinitely. We are not allowed to see
or even surmise what brings him to his tipping point. Cause and effect are
so terribly out-of-synch. It has to be that each affair, each instance of the
"widening of experience" that Dowell theorized, at the same time deepened
the wound, until he understood: things would not only go on this way,
but they would grow ever more painful, and his diminishing reserves—of
money, youth, class entitlements, and friendships—would never be enough
to save him. That he could change, turn despair to account and overcome
his own character, is somehow never felt to be an option. *This,* I think, is
the saddest part about the saddest story—Ford's apparent belief that we are
marooned in our own characters with no hope of rescue. Such pessimism
goes against everything we imbibe from our twelve-step therapeutic culture and harkens back to an old-world psychological determinism, but I
don't trust myself to make a convincing case against it.

"Live All You Can"

Henry James's *The Ambassadors*

———•———

I HAVE LAUNCHED a number of well-intentioned assaults on *The Ambassadors* since my late twenties, each time starting out with great velocity, but just as quickly getting glue on my shoes, never until just now getting past the scenes of Lambert Strether's first arrival in Paris, which come fairly early on in the book. But however frustrated I got, after a few years I was always ready to try again. I'm not sure I can explain why.

I have no such impulse toward *The Golden Bowl* or *The Wings of the Dove*. I hope I *will* one day read these late novels, of course, but I also can wait. The business with *The Ambassadors* is clearly different, and over time my failures have become interesting to me. They raise two questions. Why did I feel I had to "get" this book? And: Why did I always stop? Are the questions linked? Of course they are. In the reader's psyche everything is linked.

Probably my first exposure to James's novel was a citation in some essay of the well-known "Live all you can" peroration that Strether delivers to the oddly referenced "little Bilham" at a garden party in Paris quite early on in his stay. The cadence is so familiar—anyone who reads literary essays, never mind the James itself, will probably have encountered it: "Live all you can; it's a mistake not to. It doesn't so much matter what you do in particular, so long as you have your life. If you haven't had that what *have* you had?"

These words, like Rilke's overcited: "You must change your life," would lodge in a young man's memory. I would have read them then as James's seconding of what I already knew, putting the thrust of his civilized prestige behind what I was still translating out of the counterculture playbook, turning it into a gentleman's version of Steppenwolf's "Born to Be Wild."

Later, as I reached my late thirties, the resonance would change somewhat. For at a certain point one understands—I understood—that, to crib Boris Pasternak now, life is not a walk across a country field. As a man gaining on forty, with a wife, a young child, and a mortgage that was like a boil on my soul, I began to discover that what I had thought was this simple business of "living" was not simple at all—how at times its deeper meanings could shimmer out of reach like those cool beds of water on the highway just up ahead. But if the feeling of achieved existence proved elusive, I always believed I would be experiencing it, savoring it, soon.

During this extended gradient of first adulthood, I was still making attempts on James's text, still not breaking through, and here is the place to suggest why. For much as I was intrigued by that idea I'd seized upon—*The Ambassadors* was about daring to live fully—and much as I admired the novels of James that I *had* read, especially *The Portrait of a Lady,* and much as I wanted to take hold of what this master had folded away inside the petals of his prose, I couldn't seem to find my way in. The sentences drove me mad with their receding referents, their abstract knowingness, their absence of the granular particulars that make writers even as challenging as Virginia Woolf or Vladimir Nabokov or James Joyce such a delight to read. I found nothing of the sort in the later James—though I had remembered *The Portrait of a Lady* as being gratifyingly tangible in just these ways.

The novel is essentially woven from such recalcitrant materials, and there is no difficulty about producing an example. I plunge my thumb into the meaty bulk of my Penguin paperback and pull up, arbitrarily:

> It was quite as if he knew his surreptitious step had been divined, and it was also as if he missed the chance to explain the purity of his motive; but this privation of relief should be precisely his small penance: it was not amiss for Strether that he should find himself

to that degree uneasy. If he had been challenged or accused, rebuked for meddling or otherwise pulled up, he would probably have shown, on his own system, all the height of his consistency, all the depth of his good faith. Explicit resentment of his course would have made him take the floor, and the thump of his fist on the table would have affirmed him as consciously incorruptible. Had what now really prevailed with Strether been but a dread of that thump—a dread of wincing a little painfully at what it might invidiously demonstrate?

I apologize for not taking the time to lay out the context of this short passage. But to do so would be to go diving into the currents of implication that swirl everywhere around Strether, and this is not—here, anyway—the point. The point is just to remark on the prose style that builds a momentum of nuanced suggestiveness even as it holds the reader at a textual arm's distance, thus inducing that "irritable reaching" that John Keats proposed as somehow antithetical to the poetic apprehension.

I am more willing—now—to grant that there may be a method, or at least a point to these phrasings, that they create in the reader a sense of "almost" and make perceptible but ineffable what in fact *is* perceptible but ineffable: the inward fusion of thought and feeling that stays clear of exact articulation.

That "now" hints at a changed outlook. At last I can congratulate myself for having, on the fourth or fifth attempt, at age fifty-two, after decades of apprenticeship to "difficult" books, finally made it through. It was a victory of the will, to be sure. But not of will alone, for the will was always there, though maybe with less invested pride. This past year I finally hit a limit, telling myself, "If you can't get the novel on this go-round, you might as well give it up."

I recognized a difference this time. I felt, in the throes of my exertion, matching my concentration to the text's resistance like a driver working clutch and gas, that it was not pressure alone that was pushing me through, but something else—a psychological readiness I had lacked before. And this came from changes in my life. I was older; I was a veteran of various obscure rites of passage that I could not have imagined in my thirties or early forties. These rites had less to do with specific experiences, and more with the shifts of vantage and relation, which in turn have everything to do with my evolving sense of time and the steady lengthening of the shadow-line of memory. Looking to bring some of these awarenesses into the light, I decided to write about my experience of *The Ambassadors*.

Before I try to push through to any of these more psychological considerations, though, I want to reflect on the particular—uncommon—kind of reading that the novel requires; how it was that I had to get in synch with the prose; and how the process of making the adjustment nudged me toward all kinds of quasi (if not crazy) metaphysical considerations. Which was very likely *not* James's intention, though who can ever be sure?

In this most recent reading I was like the fabled little engine, chanting subaudibly, "I think I can, I think I can," as the text reared up like the tracks of some narrow-gauge railroad. But had it not been for a certain intriguing anomaly I might not have made it.

As a reader, I can't abide the irritation of partial comprehension. I can't make myself go forward if I feel in arrears to what I am reading. And nothing trips me up more than abstractions. Through whatever bent of my psychological makeup, I have a hard time assigning any but the most provisional status to the counters that go with concepts and states of feeling. Maybe I am not alone in this. When I read, in the passage I quoted, the following sentence—"If he had been challenged or accused, rebuked for meddling or otherwise pulled up, he would probably have shown, on his own system, all the height of his consistency, all the depth of his good faith."—I immediately go to war with my own uneasiness. I flounder. My mind shuttles recursively between the assertion and the implied situation—a situation that, in James, has likely not had its material contours filled—and I lurch clumsily (so it feels) between one part of the sentence and the other, parsing syntax, clarifying antecedents, bearing down to make sure I have extracted as much as I can before moving on. But all too often when I *do* move on, it's with a sense of what the poststructuralists called "deferral."

That said, what allowed me to keep reading was the discovery, this time, of a very particular delayed effect, what felt to me like the textual equivalent of stepping back from a pointillist painting regarded too closely and having the flurry of dots and dabs coalesce into a sensible shape. If *The Ambassadors* was consistently blurry on initial impact, it seemed to gather to a kind of clarity behind me. To be sure, I couldn't always see Strether—or young Chad Newsome, his quarry, or the various women who created such a gauze of consequence around both of them—in the way I like to see characters, but page by page I felt how, through this strange crystallizing effect, I was pulled in closer to the man's state of mind, his moral and emotional being.

I explain this by suggesting that there is a mysterious dynamic of accumulation in the prose, a delayed-reaction effect in which each new scene or disclosure brings forward some suggestion that had been left latent before, maybe deliberately. One example would be the very gradual revelation of Strether's ambivalence about his assignment to rescue Chad from the temptations of old civilization. I had to appreciate the extent of this ambivalence through later passages before I could begin to resolve some of the puzzling intimations given earlier. The retroactive firming up of things certainly helped me stay the course. In fact, these delayed apprehensions, when they came, felt more lasting than easier kinds of apprehensions; they were like something won back from obscurity.

Reading *The Ambassadors* was still in many ways a penance, undertaken not so much for pleasure, but because I felt it was good for me, because I wanted to redeem my failures and have it be a book I *had* read—I wanted to validate my membership ticket for the club of serious readers. But there was also the hope, planted by my earliest exposures, that the novel might hold some important secret for me, some clues about living.

As it turned out, while James did offer me a good deal of information about life, it was nothing like what I had imagined. This was not the stuff of college English papers—no tidy themes. Beyond the neatly wrapped Strether wisdom—"Live all you can"—there was not much that I could extract. The insights were, rather, embedded or, better, woven through; they were lived recognitions that I could weigh and reckon, testing them against what I knew or imagined. At the same time, they made certain things about getting older considerably more clear to me: this was the subtle fruit of all that penance.

My response had much to do with the nature of the novel, its conception and construction, its resolute refusal of conventional plot. This is not to say that plot in itself produces exportable sorts of wisdom—message units of meaning—but pitched orchestrations of plot *do* create the tensions that generate situations of revelation. And while *The Ambassadors* does move in its final chapters toward a climax of sorts—Strether, away from Paris, surprises Chad in the company of Marie de Vionnet, his married "friend," and realizes the true nature of their entanglement—the encounter delivers only the most muted charge. By this point Strether very nearly knows the truth; and the moment does not disrupt his own trajectory, but merely hastens it.

James's deployment of plot is willfully uninflected. It is as if he had set himself the task of stretching the material of civilized—that is to say "nondramatic"—negotiations as far as he could over his few vertical poles of incident. Compared to *The Ambassadors,* any novel by Jane Austen, who was only slightly less civilized than the Master, reads like a fever chart of the human passions.

A paragraph should be enough to summarize the major "action" of the novel. At the instigation of one Mrs. Newsome, a wealthy widow with whom he has a relationship (doubtless a Jamesian relationship) and an understanding (if he succeeds they will marry), Lambert Strether travels to Europe—first England, then France—to disentangle her son from his Continental influences and bring him home to Woollett (Connecticut), where he is wanted at the helm of the family business. (The premise was used, with dark and interesting variation, by Patricia Highsmith in *The Talented Mr. Ripley*). Arriving in Paris, entering into Chad's social networks, Strether feels his original sense of mission slipping away. He is drawn by the more liberal and cultivated sensibilities, by Chad's artistic friend, "little Bilham," and by women like Maria Gostrey and Marie de Vionnet. There follow hundreds of pages chronicling his ambassadorial feints and the subtle undermining of his resolve. When Mrs. Newsome's daughter, the fearsome Mrs. Pocock, and her husband, arrive to force the moment, Strether realizes how much his desires and needs have changed. His surprise encounter with Chad and Marie, which is, yes, sexually inflected, clarifies to him that his assignment has become pointless. Even more pointless to him is the world—his former life—from whence that assignment originated. At novel's end, Strether, a man in his midfifties, is very much at the end of something, with no clear sense of whether any more beginnings are in the offing.

Such a sketch omits all of the textured layers that make up the body of the novel. But at the same time it suggests how little outward definition is needed. Or, to put it another way, how rich and pliable is the stuff of human interaction, so long as we understand it as happening within a strictly bounded—constrained—field of action. In James this means accepting a strict adherence to an assumed social morality. Only this constraint allows the finely discriminated play of decision and consequence to resonate. If you were to remove the grid of social codes, to set the scene in an arena governed by moral relativism, the whole structure would collapse in on itself. Strether's sighting of Chad and Marie has to be seen—and felt—as scandalous, or else nothing about the novel makes much sense. That it *does* strike us as scandalous testifies to the power of art to immerse us deeply in what has with the passing of time become a largely alien moral order.

But if it was not a specific message or set of realizations that I took away from my reading of *The Ambassadors,* what was my payoff? What made the reading worth the many hours it took? The question interests me. For I have no hesitation now about marking the experience out as worthy, even important, both on the immediate "process" level, but even more in terms of what the great Italian poet Eugenio Montale called "the second life of art," referring to the ways in which a work lives in us after we have finished our looking, listening, or reading. Indeed, for me the value of the novel lies mainly in its aftereffects, the residues it has left behind—residues that become subtle goads to new awareness.

The more immediate effects of the novel obviously have a great deal to do with deceleration, the knot-unraveling discipline that prolongs itself sentence to sentence as the mind grapples with James's refined but convoluted syntax. There are always the local satisfactions, like the ego-boosting sense of mastery that comes as headway is made, as density yields, and if it doesn't often yield completely, there is still the tantalizing sensation of being on the verge. The pleasure here is directly related to the faith that psychological profundities await. Fortunately, with James the glimpses are intense enough—and come often enough—to keep this expectation alive.

I won't presume that this is true for everyone, but the committed reader has to be at some level addicted to the complexities of linguistic entanglement, to the release of whatever literary endorphins the stressing of the language centers produces. Steady focus can be gratifying in itself, and certainly James compels that. Moreover, when this focus is directed not upon facts or formulae, but on the ever-shifting atmospheres of relationship, on the play of emotion and intent, desire and surmise, all of which elude clear definition, the effect is singular. Although for long stretches I was confused, I was also thrilled. If I didn't pick up all the signals, I was still very much aware that signaling was intense all around me. I felt like a recent immigrant arriving in a room full of native speakers.

All of this was at times exhilarating, yet if at the end it had only been this, I would not think of it as a profound literary experience. But finally, in spite of—or because of—the fact that his diffuse narrative built to no major climax, James managed to shake me deeply. So much, I would say, that *The Ambassadors* will stand as one of the private touchstones of this more relatively retrospective time of life.

The reason, however, is not so easily named or anatomized. Occasioned and conditioned by my immersion in the novel, half-concealed there like some carpet figure, it is itself somehow distinctively Jamesian.

THROUGH WHATEVER OBSCURE SEQUENCING of scenes and finessing of transitions, through the subtly graded shifts in the inner life of Strether, James managed to evoke in me the sharpest awarenesses of how we accommodate the passing of time. Reading, I recognized how we can inch forward day by day in what feels like one sustained state until, mysteriously, some critical mass is achieved, some exit velocity, and we feel we have come through to the other side of something—what had been the unquestioned *ongoing* has receded to become one of our epochs. We have grown, or changed, and that long extended *now,* with a slight twist of vantage, becomes the past. More, by becoming past in this way the experience begins to feel slightly unreal to us, and this recognition puts everything into play. Life stands revealed again: it is provisional, poignant, fraught.

Strether is deep in his middle years when he is thus stripped of his shell and reborn to circumstance. The question of the novel is how he will survive into a full new life, or whether, failing that, he will become one of the many who turn back and wall themselves up in the bygone. He has the resource to escape the pull of Mrs. Newsome and what she represents, but does he have the additional resource to build himself up from the ground independently? James leaves the reader wondering, possibly fearing the worst.

James's re-creation of the passing of time, the movement of a man from stage to stage, is achieved with the lightest touch. His way of setting one tone alongside another, the very gradual darkening of tints, makes me think of the application of washes of watercolor to a sheet of densely textured paper. But for all that delicacy of presentation, it still affected me powerfully.

The movement of narrative represents a condensation of time and can often deliver a strong emotion of loss. At the end of many good novels I feel almost heartbroken, and it is usually for this reason. I am leaving behind what has been an intense experience. But with James the effect is intensified as means and ends converge. The whole point of *The Ambassadors* is that an era in a man's life has concluded, and by refusing any strong suggestion of what the future holds for Strether, James amplifies the hard uncertainty of all such passages.

We are left at novel's end with an unsettled feeling about Strether's fate. So much of his past has receded and taken on the sepia tones of melancholic contemplation. The mood is deepened, made almost painful by the fact that he has so little expectation left. His affections have been undermined, shocked into retraction.

My response to *The Ambassadors* had everything to do with my tacit

identification with Strether—not with his morality or his emotional reti-
cence (though some of that charge would surely stick), but with his reflective mode of addressing experience—which was James's own mode. I felt
enough connected to the character that when he experienced his great realization that an era—possibly the last era of possibility—had passed, I felt
the bitter tug in my own gut, as if it were no accident that I had resolved
to read the novel right when I did, as if the whole experience was meant to
throw a light on what has to be one of the darker transitions of adult life.

I am being melodramatic, I realize that. I'm not suggesting that I have
turned some last corner, or that for me, as possibly for Strether, there is
nothing to do but play out the hand. But I do believe that I have arrived
now at some preliminary stage, one that plays out in lowercase themes
that will later be capitalized.

If I sound tentative or vague, it's because I am looking for a way to
avoid the standard midlife clichés. But these feelings come to all of us
who are lucky enough to live so long. They accompany the ultimately
unavoidable realization that our basic relation to time—which is to say to
possibility, to memory—has changed. The former diminishes as the latter
grows, and there is nothing to be done. At a certain point in adulthood
the weights seem equally distributed, the balance is at rest. And then, a
moment later, it begins to tip, imperceptibly at first, then more obviously.

For me, then, there was a fitting interleaving of book and life. I may
have encouraged the event by choosing to return to the book when I did,
suspecting that this time I would be more attuned to its preoccupations
and subdued delivery. Certainly the work of reading was a gradual priming of the self, as James pulled me in and steadily brought me around
to his sense of things. So that even though it was hard to get purchase
on the character of Strether—he is no Harry Angstrom, no Humbert
Humbert—I could feel my subjectivity, my reading self, merging with
the edges of his cloudy being. This is not exactly identification. I didn't
walk around half-convinced I was Strether, but I was in his, and therefore
James's, sphere of magnetic influence.

As I neared the last pages of *The Ambassadors,* when Strether has weath-
ered the crisis over his mission and realizes that the valence of his entire ex-

perience has changed, I found myself inadvertently tuned up. As Strether prepared to confront the falling away—the loss—of a whole epoch of experience, I was, coincidentally or not, set up for a parallel moment in my own life.

The business is obviously complex, inwardly muddy, not to be represented through one realization or shudder of awakening, but there was one surprisingly intense instance of intersection, art crossing into life, which may begin to suggest how these personal reckonings arrive.

I had been reading the novel for several weeks—pacing myself, but also *being* paced by the opaque-seeming density of it all—and had brought it along to Bennington, to the writing residency I attend every January (and June), determined to finish it there, away from work and family.

And so I did, early one morning, sitting by myself in the barren downstairs of the house I'd been assigned. I knew as I hovered in that suspended state that comes before the decisive closing of the covers, that it was reaching me with a finer accuracy than anything I'd read in a long time. I could not say how, quite, except that I felt stirred up, pulled toward that melancholic thinking that has worked in my life like an undertow for decades. My mood on finishing the James was ruefully reflective, tinged with recognitions about time and mutability. I felt some of the intangible profundity that comes often when I end my involvement with a writer's world. But this time I also experienced a distinct sense of vantage, as if my contemplation of passage and change could take in my entire life.

I walked around in this state for some hours, thinking on the big picture and dwelling in the most general and obvious way on transience. But in the end it was the specific that turned the knife. I remember the moment perfectly. It was a bitingly cold afternoon. The fading light and the snow reflected the atmosphere of the well-known Childe Hassam painting of the Boston Common. I was hurrying along, making the transit between the library and the road that would take me back down to the house. I gave a sidelong glance—as I did every time I passed—at the little walled-in courtyard just adjacent to the library. The entryway was open, with a view of the concrete bench set off at the back. I had a special association with that bench. Sitting there one morning several summers ago, reading student essays, I'd had one of those minor visitations, a moment when I looked up at the trees around me and all of a sudden felt myself stripped free of my daily life and filled with some higher brand of energy. I knew, for a short while, that I was in the right place, and I knew why and how what I did mattered. Although it wasn't quite W. B. Yeats's tea-shop vision—when he felt at once that he was blessed and "could bless"— the moment had its own special light.

Still walking, still girding myself against the cold, I constructed the image—myself sitting there—formally, from the outside. And then came the shift, the inward flip. Just like that, with no helping push, no willed intensification, I caught hold of it from the other side. From within. I felt—even in the subzero weather—the memory pressure of summer, the morning air on my skin. I sensed, or somehow knew, the rustle of the papers I had set down there, weighting them with my palm. That was all. There was a little flash, one of those simultaneously delicious and painful bracketings. The *then* moment and the *now* moment, and between the two some wobbling vertigo that lasted at most for the rest of my short walk. For of course these feelings don't stay; they turn into the thoughts we have about them.

I went back to the house and sat with those sensations-become-thoughts and I circled back to thinking about Strether and the end of the novel and realizing, as I went through the sequences of his visit to Paris, his mission, that something very similar happens to him.

I have looked up the passage, and now, not surprisingly it signifies very differently. The whole process makes a strange circle. For it could just be that these very pages—the feeling of them, anyway—were what set me up for my moment. And now, that strange little rush behind me, I look back to the novel and find my response intensified, given new texture. But then, isn't this circuit shuttle between book and life the real point of our reading?

In the scene, Strether, nearing the end of his stay in Paris, goes to pay a last visit to Chad, and as he approaches the apartment he experiences a striking echo of his first visit, at which time he spied the figure who would turn out to be young Bilham having a cigarette on the third-floor balcony. Now:

He had since had occasion, a few times, to pass the house without going in; but he had never passed it without again feeling how it had then spoken to him. He stopped short tonight on coming to sight of it: it was as if his last day were oddly copying his first. The windows of Chad's apartment were open to the balcony—a pair of them lighted; and a figure that had come out and taken up little Bilham's attitude, a figure whose cigarette-spark he could see leaned on the rail and looked down at him.

For the reader, as for Strether himself, the collapse of one moment upon another—it is too trite and limiting to call it "Proustian"—creates the frame for the central recognition: not only has a significant period of time elapsed, but the "click" of the second sighting somehow marks the line of a distinct era. The recent period, with its hopes, affections, and psychological subterfuges—its emotional narrative—has come to a close; it has been rounded off. It has also begun to slip away in time. And as it does—as we remark the shift—a great sadness rises up. For Strether, but for ourselves as well.

Do I presume? Maybe we all contend with the passing of time in our lives differently. All I know is that the sensation of time moving through its very different seasons is deeply familiar. In the case of *The Ambassadors*— and here is my realization—I had two separate, successive responses. First there was loss, both in my reaction to Strether's situation and through my own strong identification. The morning on the bench, briefly repossessed, belonged to the completed part of the past. It was marked off from the life of the present, and the recovery of those sensations was enough to confirm for me that I had indeed passed on to a new state of awareness. I had the sad jolt of "never again" as well as the recognition that my life was a long succession of many such finished eras, and that, certainly, the state of the present would sooner or later be another.

But the second understanding, the one that to some degree redeems the first, came only after the mood of the first had spent itself. The heartening thing—and maybe it marks the coming of some genuine maturity of outlook—was that I saw how those losses, those vanished feeling-states, were only in one sense losses; they were at the same time, all together, the accumulated stuff of life itself. I took it all in as a poetic image, and as soon as I had it calmed me. At that instant I saw myself as cross-sectioned, like a tree inscribed with concentric rings, each distinct, the edges darker where winter has hardened the fiber, separating one year from the next, but all packed together in an essential progress, all adding up. A fancy, perhaps *too* fancy of an extrapolation from the story of Lambert Strether in Paris, but don't we all take what we can get—or what we need—from the books that find their way to us?

Into the Blue Paint

Virginia Woolf's *To the Lighthouse*

———·———

I MMERSING MYSELF in the prose of *To the Lighthouse*, I have moments when I can't believe my good fortune at being allowed, at my own pace and discretion, for my own entirely selfish ends, to just drink up these sentences, these little streams of electric sensation, trusting each one absolutely, knowing, as is so rarely true, that the writer is completely in control; she is able to track the most nuanced stirrings of consciousness and remind us how the mind, or psyche, can hover and dive, thicken and thin out, but also loop on itself, touching its own past, holding images and feelings up for inspection like so many intricate curios picked up in a cluttered shop.

Virginia Woolf wrote of this novel in her diary that she wanted it to be full of the presence of the sea ("the sea is to be heard all through it"), and so it is, from James Ramsay's excited imagining of an expedition by boat to the lighthouse—*to the lighthouse*—on the very first page, to the artist Lily Briscoe's staring out into the "blue haze" at the very end, just before her final moment of decision about her painting. But as the sea serves as the sound track, if not the outright emblem, of the soul's unrest, of Time, of nearly any elusive element we might name, its presence touches everything with a profound dreaminess, loosening edges, lending its shadow, its percussive lulling rumble to the "moments of being" Woolf creates.

This last phrase is the title of a small collection of Woolf's autobiographical sketches, a collection that shows Woolf studying her family

and her early years of growing up from an entirely different angle. For as
any reader of Woolf knows, *To the Lighthouse* is in significant ways a re-
casting of the circumstances and sensations of her earliest years, when her
family summered at St. Ives. The characters of the parents, Mr. and Mrs.
Ramsay, are clearly modeled on her own parents, and Woolf confides as
much in her diary ("This is going to be fairly short; to have father's character done complete in it; and mother's; and St. Ives; and childhood; and all
the usual things I try to put in—life, death, etc."). The core psychological
trauma of the novel, the death within parentheses of Mrs. Ramsay in the
lyrically impersonal middle section, "Time Passes," reflects the trauma of
Virginia's adolescent loss of her mother. The writing of the novel was, by
her own account, a profound passage. As she revealed in her memoir-essay
"A Sketch of the Past": "It is perfectly true that she obsessed me, in spite of
the fact that she died when I was thirteen, until I was forty-four. . . . But
I wrote the book very quickly; and when it was written, I ceased to be obsessed by my mother. I no longer hear her voice; I do not see her."

But none of this is essential for a full reading of the novel—it may
even prove distracting if we begin trying to map the created to the "actual." The text by itself is work enough. Indeed, though I don't remember exactly when I first read *To the Lighthouse*—I was somewhere in my
midtwenties—I do have a clear recollection of how I struggled, trying
to hold character and point of view steady in my mind, anxious at the
thought of all that I might be missing, intimidated, I suppose, by the
book's aura of the canonical. Going back now, I see what a better reader
I have become, at least in the sense of hearing the music of the prose,
and feeling the time shifts and dilations of memory as revelations rather
than as tests to be passed. I suppose I've gradually trained myself to this
kind of prose. I'm certainly more aware of the flow of subjective Time in
my own life—I think of it now as one of the core enigmas of living, and
I'm avid to see how Woolf deals with it. Have I come closer to catching
hold of meaning and purpose? No. But there is less irritable reaching. I
understand better how things—situations and relationships—are seldom,
if ever, pushed to resolution, at least resolution in the sense I imagined
when I was younger. Closure does not happen out there. It is—I can picture my father tapping his head with his finger—*in here.*

I first got news of *To the Lighthouse* through my college girlfriend Jess. It was her favorite novel, a touchstone in so many of her conversations about art and relationships and family. If I didn't hurry to read it then it was because she had already planted her flags all over it, and given our complicated intellectual rivalry, an easy exchange of views would have been difficult.

The novel was freighted for Jess. She thought that Mrs. Ramsay was her mother, the atmosphere of the Ramsay home was a distillation of what she had grown up with, and so on. To me it seemed all too precious and domestic. I liked rougher, more overtly existential stuff—my Henry Miller, my Blaise Cendrars, my Jean Genet—and I liked it served straight-up.

I only read *To the Lighthouse* years later, long after Jess and I had parted ways, when I no longer believed that every scene would make me think of her, or that the setting would bring back too vividly the time we had lived together next to the ocean on the coast of Maine. But I was fooling myself. These feelings and sensations never just go away, and when I finally took my turn with Jess's favorite book, they all came flinging at me. Every passage was somehow filtered through the screen of her old adoration. It was as close as I had ever come, I thought, to capturing her way of seeing the world, and it was too late to avail me anything.

But this is not an essay about indulging old romantic business. It is about *To the Lighthouse*. And here the interesting thing is that just as the novel could, at one point, feel saturated through every line with the presence of another, so it could, after the passage of more years, after that necessary first reading, emerge sea-cleansed, once again become just words on the page, the evocation not of my past but of the life of the Ramsays. I don't have a clue how this works.

THE OBVIOUS BRILLIANCE of *To the Lighthouse* is found in Woolf's uncanny deployment of lyrical prose to evoke—and enact—the seemingly infinite motions, and gradations of motion, of consciousness, an undertaking that is challenging in itself, but becomes breathtakingly so when the point of view is distributed among several vantages and the time frame is broken to convey a privately *and* historically important passage of time. Had I written about the novel several years ago, I probably would have made this my central focus, but now, for whatever reasons, I am far more drawn to the exploration of its wisdoms. I want to loot the book for my own selfish purposes.

I am, I know this, in search of certain kinds of solace these days. Much as I did when I was in my teens and first reading seriously, I want to find understandings—information—that I can import into my living, not the daily side, with its high-speed shuttling between tasks and obligations, but what I feel is there when I open my eyes in the early morning dark and the old questions assault me. Where most novels I read, so many of them smart and pleasure-strewn, don't address more than a corner of this ancient preoccupation with being, *To the Lighthouse* comes at it frontally.

Thinking about Woolf's novel, as I have been doing for several weeks now, I realize that there are several preoccupations I keep returning to. And though I don't usually like writing essays that proceed by enumerated stages, I can't seem to help myself here: I feel challenged, at times almost overwhelmed by Woolf's intense fluidity, by the surge of perception, reflection, and recollection that pushes her outwardly simple narrative forward. I don't believe that I can do it justice on its own terms; I need to isolate the main thematic strands that have woven their way into my reflective life. To separate them out is misleading: just a few inches under the surface all of Woolf's roots are grown together.

THE FIRST OF THESE PREOCCUPATIONS is introduced right away, in the book's second paragraph, as six-year-old James Ramsay is busily cutting out pictures from an illustrated catalogue and asking his mother if he will be able to go on an expedition to the lighthouse planned for the next day. His mother's reassuring words are, in fact, the novel's opening: "'Yes, of course, if it's fine tomorrow.'" Mrs. Ramsay sounds the note of care even as she allows for the provisionality of all such expectation. Writes Woolf:

> Since he belonged, even at the age of six, to that great clan which
> cannot keep this feeling separate from that, but must let future
> prospects, with their joys and sorrows, cloud what is actually at
> hand, since to such people even in earliest childhood any turn in

the wheel of sensation has the power to crystallise and transfix the moment upon which its gloom or radiance rests, James Ramsay, sitting on the floor cutting out pictures from the illustrated catalogue of the Army and Navy Stores, endowed the picture of a refrigerator, as his mother spoke, with heavenly bliss.

Quite a first mouthful, but one that is crucial to the novel and the inquiry—or argument—it seeks to carry out. For this impulse of the self-uncensored six-year-old represents in essence, the idea of reality as irradiated by subjectivity, the world—to slap a philosophical tag on it—as will and representation, as a credible figment of our own projections. James is identified as belonging to a type, one of those who cannot help but view all circumstance through the scrim of self, configured by their own affective temper. And James is here but his mother's ambassador, an unreconstructed version of what she manifestly is.

Against the subjective—opposing it at the most basic level, but also bound to it in one of those missing-ion kinds of bonds—is the worldview of Mr. Ramsay, the philosopher-father. He is, before anything else, presented to us as the logical naysayer, the discouraging spirit whose first utterance, hard on the heels of James's expressed longing, is: "'But . . . it won't be fine.'" Yes, no—and between the poles we find a marriage, a family, and a complex and varied domestic life.

Mr. Ramsay—we learn this within pages—is a thinker, a theoretical materialist who feels that he has, in the alphabet of rational progress, attained perhaps to the letter Q. But if this represents a failure, and for him it does, there is at least the consolation that very few have gotten even that far. His focus? "'Subject and object and the nature of reality,'" is how Andrew, one of his sons, describes it to Lily Briscoe, who in these early pages is shown to be working on a portrait of Mrs. Ramsay and James as they sit together. "'Think of a kitchen table,'" he tells her, "'when you're not there.'"

Subject and object and the nature of reality: these are the central investigations of the novel as well. We see—again, this is the first thematic thread—both the intellectual irreconcilability of Mr. and Mrs. Ramsay, in their fundamental perceptions of reality, but also the powerful irrational attraction they each have for one another based, in part, on what each of them lack. We find evidence of this indispensable conjunction everywhere in the novel—most in the emotional bereavement Mr. Ramsay feels after Mrs. Ramsay's death, which we sense is not just for the loss of the beloved, but also for the sustaining atmosphere she created, an absence at his intellectual core.

Much earlier, however, in what is probably the first real expression of this, we are shown how Mrs. Ramsay all but mesmerizes Charles Tansley, Mr. Ramsay's visiting disciple, called "the atheist" by the children, when he accompanies her on a walk to town. It is not a direct philosophical recognition that Tansley has. Rather, he finds himself gradually and obscurely overwhelmed by her presence, her way of situating herself in the world. They have gone together to the house of a woman whom Mrs. Ramsay regularly visits. She leaves Tansley for a short time, then returns, bringing him a sudden onslaught of feeling and recognition:

> He heard her quick step above; heard her voice cheerful, then low; looked at the mats, tea-caddies, glass shades; waited quite impatiently; looked forward eagerly to the walk home; determined to carry her bag; then heard her come out; shut a door; say they must keep the windows open and the doors shut, ask at the house for anything they wanted (she must be talking to a child) when, suddenly, in she came, stood for a moment silent (as if she had been pretending up there, and for a moment let herself be now), stood quite motionless for a moment against a picture of Queen Victoria wearing the blue ribbon of the Garter; when all at once he realised that it was this: it was this:—she was the most beautiful person he had ever seen.

Throughout the novel, especially in the first section, we hear of Mrs. Ramsay's beauty, an attribute we quickly realize is less about her physical appearance—though by all accounts she is still a very distinguished-looking older woman—and more about a kind of emanation. Mrs. Ramsay has a rare way of galvanizing her surroundings, of influencing the perceptions and feelings of others, drawing them together into consonance. This power—even Mr. Ramsay, so committed to the project of disinterested thought, feels it—manifests itself to others as an aura of beauty. This is what has Mr. Ramsay so enthralled at section's end, when, after dinner is over—his wife has presided over an especially convivial gathering—he watches her standing at the window of the study. Woolf deftly manipulates perspective so that Mr. Ramsay's thoughts join almost imperceptibly with Mrs. Ramsay's own suppositions, the effect of which is a complex grappling of need and adoration expressing the peculiar merging of their separate selves.

The remarkable penultimate paragraph begins with Mrs. Ramsay's sense of obstacle: "For she felt that he was still looking at her, but that his look had changed. He wanted something—wanted the thing she always found it so difficult to give him; wanted her to tell him that she loved him. And that, no, she could not do." Then, a moment later: "She knew that he was thinking, You are more beautiful than ever. And she felt herself very beautiful." Finally, with another of those Woolfian modulations that capture so uncannily the shape-shifting thrusts of the inner life, she brings what has been twisting and turning between them to conclusion:

> Then, knowing that he was watching her, instead of saying anything she turned, holding her stocking, and looked at him. And as she looked at him she began to smile, for though she had not said a word, he knew, of course he knew, that she loved him. He could not deny it. And smiling she looked out of the window and said (thinking to herself, Nothing on earth can equal this happiness)—"Yes, you were right. It's going to be wet tomorrow. You won't be able to go." And she looked at him smiling. For she had triumphed again. She had not said it: yet he knew.

I have been generous with quotation, but with some writers there is no other way—their process is so shaded, so incremental, so embodied in the rhythmic pulse of the language that descriptive characterization is very difficult. As for the wisdom of all this: it comes down to that

core theme, of "subject and object and the nature of reality." Woolf uses
Mrs. Ramsay to affirm, counter Mr. Ramsay's labored assertions to the
contrary, that our reality is in many ways our own projection—our will
and representation—and that it is not entirely absurd to speak of the self
in terms of the soul. We certainly feel that Mrs. Ramsay is a soul—not
just through her registered thoughts and responses, but through the reactions of the people around her, and, later, through the sense of palpable
absence her death creates.

A second thematic fascination, related to the first, has to do with
Woolf's idea of moments of being, which she has elaborated in her autobiographical essay, "A Sketch of the Past," written in 1940, where it serves
as the basis of her own writer's phenomenology. She sets down a crucial
opposition, between experience that matters and experience that doesn't.
The latter she characterizes as "a kind of nondescript cotton wool." She
explains: "A great part of every day is not lived consciously. One walks,
eats, sees things, deals with what has to be done; the broken vacuum
cleaner; ordering dinner; writing orders to Mabel. . . ." Against these, her
"moments of being" emerge as exceptional; they are shocks that lift us
into awareness. Speaking as an artist, she writes:

> . . . I go on to suppose that the shock-receiving capacity is what
> makes me a writer. I hazard the explanation that a shock is at once
> in my case followed by the desire to explain it. I feel that I have
> had a blow; but it is not, as I thought as a child, simply a blow
> from an enemy hidden behind the cotton wool of daily life; it is
> or will become a revelation of some order; it is a token of some
> real thing behind appearances; and I make it real by putting it
> into words. . . . From this I reach what I might call a philosophy;
> at any rate it is a constant idea of mine; that behind the cotton
> wool is hidden a pattern; that we—I mean all human beings—are
> connected with this; that the whole world is a work of art; that we
> are parts of the work of art.

When I read a passage like this, I feel lit up. No dramatic rendering,
no tour de force of description brings me closer to the feeling that this

is the truth of experience. I find it secreted in a rambling memoir-essay and marvel that it isn't somewhere framed and on exhibit. That flashing spark of connection and the giddy sense of enlargement it brings—*that the whole world is a work of art; that we are parts of the work of art*—it confirms for me, not that I ever really doubted it, that literature is my best bet for secular enlightenment.

Although Mrs. Ramsay is not a philosopher like her husband, or an artist like Lily Briscoe, she is no less profound an individual than either. It is her genius to distill these "moments of being" from the murk of ordinary experience, and by doing so—doing so in such a way that they are recognized by those around her—she testifies with her whole person to the idea of this underlying pattern of meaning.

But how are such moments to be distilled? What special insight or aptitude does Mrs. Ramsay possess? Obviously there is no formula—if there were the world would have been remade long since. It is a matter of instincts and intuitions, of one's having an extreme receptivity to the revealed and concealed feelings of others, of exerting the particular magnetism that draws the scattered energies (or vibrations) of any situation toward a single center and brings them to clear articulation. But the gift works fitfully. Like Woolf's other great heroine, Clarissa Dalloway, who gives herself to the making of a party like an artist willing a work of art into existence, Mrs. Ramsay encounters repeated frustrations and obstacles. Her world is by no means a single sustained moment. Indeed, to look at her fussing with her children or her houseguests, you would not think she had *any* special art or secret. But as the event of the dinner affirms, she is the supreme hostess—not in the conventional, but in the exalted sense. With her looks, gestures, responses—with her strength of presence—she guides those around her toward a recognition of occasion, nothing less than a shared and very nearly religious sense of communion. Although there are many at the table, and although each exchange obeys its own dynamic, somehow it is Mrs. Ramsay who is responsible for the convergence of forces with which the event concludes.

At meal's end, after Mr. Ramsay has recited a poem, the old poet, Augustus Carmichael, stands up and finds a way to turn that recitation into a benediction:

But the voice stopped. She looked round. She made herself get
up. Augustus Carmichael had risen and, holding his table napkin
so that it looked like a long white robe he stood chanting:
To see the Kings go riding by
Over lawn and daisy lea
With their palm leaves and cedar sheaves
    Luriana, Lurilee

And as she passed him, he turned slightly towards her repeat-
ing the last words:

    Luriana, Lurilee

And bowed to her as if he did her homage. Without knowing
why, she felt that he liked her better than he had ever done before;
and with a feeling of relief and gratitude she returned his bow and
passed through the door which he held open for her.

Woolf's moment, then, might be defined as life gathered to a semblance
of permanence, its ember blown up to a glow, in the light of which we
glimpse part of a larger pattern. And if we don't make out the design itself,
we are at least reassured, or reminded, that there is such a thing underlying the seemingly unstructured succession of events. A moment may
have archetypal character, but it may also be nothing more than a shock
that recalls a person to a larger perspective—that radiating sense of life as a
mystery that we all sometimes experience. In this it resembles the Joycean
idea of the "epiphany," the distinguishing characteristic of which is the ordinariness of the circumstance from which it arises.

However much the Woolfian moment shines or vividly adheres in
memory, it cannot survive beyond that unless it is taken up and transformed by the artistic process, and this is a third thematic thread. We find
evidence of the memory obsession throughout the novel. Mrs. Ramsay at
one point recalls her visit to the Mannings, old friends, and one of these
moments:

Never should she forget Herbert killing a wasp with a teaspoon on the bank! And it was still going on, Mrs. Ramsay mused, gliding like a ghost among the chairs and tables of that drawing-room on the banks of the Thames where she had been so very, very cold twenty years ago; but now she went among them like a ghost; and it fascinated her, as if, while she had changed, that particular day, now become very still and beautiful, had remained there, all these years.

Such is the power of memory, and such is its human extent: to create in the person the sensation of vanished circumstance living on. And such is the power of certain moments to gather to themselves so intense a charge. But Mrs. Ramsay dies, and with her all the ghosts of memories she has gathered. Take away the perceiver and the perceived world disappears—unless, like Mr. Ramsay's table, it has some independent existence. This is humanly unbearable to contemplate, hence the consolation of philosophy and the consolation of art.

The later pages of the novel, after the "Time Passes" interlude, in which we learn of the death of Mrs. Ramsay and two of her children (Prue and Andrew) and the catastrophic fact of the war, belong significantly to Lily Briscoe, the painter. Throughout the first section we have been aware of Lily—hers is one of the voices—first as she attempts to paint a portrait of Mrs. Ramsay and James, and later as she sits with the others at dinner, taking small part in the conversation, but also brooding on her work, attempting without success to solve a painterly problem. Her preoccupation, as Woolf presents it, is strictly formal, having to do with the distribution of shapes on the canvas, a search for balance that would seem at first to be even less connected to sensuous and affective life than Mr. Ramsay's abstruse meditations. She gives an enormous amount of thought to the placement of a particular tree, for instance, and even when she is at the dinner table, the tree is in her thoughts. Staring at her fellow guest William Bankes, with whom she feels a certain connection, a connection Mrs. Ramsay imagines might become something more, she finds her thoughts suddenly triggered back to her project:

She remembered, all of a sudden as if she had found a treasure, that she had her work. In a flash she saw her picture, and thought, Yes, I shall put the tree further in the middle; then I shall avoid that awkward space. That's what I shall do. That's what has been puzzling me. She took up the salt cellar and put it down again on a flower in pattern in the table-cloth, so as to remind herself to move the tree.

But Lily is not cut from the philosopher's cloth; in terms of registering the human undercurrents, she is much closer to Mrs. Ramsay. Indeed, her desire to paint Mrs. Ramsay and James is a gesture of profound admiration and love. She appreciates the woman's mysterious being, and her wrestling with shape and color is not a denial of primary human forces, but reflects her artist's determination to present them through abstract painterly equivalences. The effort presupposes the existence of an underlying absolute pattern and assumes that visual forms can discover and express it. Just as Paul Cézanne did not so much paint apples as he used apples as a pretext for exploring the dynamics of perception, so Lily is determined to use shape and color to testify to human alignments that transcend the instability of the passing hour.

The transformational nature of artistic perception fascinates Woolf, and she explores it throughout the novel by way of Lily's perceptions of the world around her. At one point, for instance, she is walking with Bankes, and they see Mr. and Mrs. Ramsay standing together watching their children, Prue and Jaspar, throwing a ball back and forth:

And suddenly the meaning which, for no reason at all, as perhaps they are stepping out of the Tube or ringing a doorbell, descends on people, making them symbolical, making them representative, came upon them, and made them in the dusk standing, looking, the symbols of marriage, husband and wife. Then, after an instant, the symbolical outline which transcended the real figures sank down again, and they became, as they met them, Mr. and Mrs. Ramsay watching the children throwing catches.

There can be no simple playing with shapes and colors for this woman. She is at every moment working at world and representation as if they are two sides of an equation that must be solved once and for all. In the first half of the book this solution persistently eludes her. She reproaches herself with not seeing clearly enough, for lacking mastery. But maybe what is needed is just the passing of Time itself, the withdrawal of presence into memory, where it can become subject to the inscrutable refining work of the unconscious. How else to account for Lily's eventual triumph, the moment when all figures and variables fall into place, and the solution is a matter of a single confident stroke of the brush?

The novel's last section, "The Lighthouse," gives compact lyrical expression to the creative act, nominally painting, but implicitly writing as well. As with the opening section, Woolf tells the story of a single day, a day that plays off two very different events, each representing a triumph of a sort. The first of these is the expedition to the lighthouse, finally undertaken ten years later, with an aged Mr. Ramsay accompanying his two grown children, Cam and James, in a small boat. The second shows Lily beginning afresh on the painting she had conceived all those years ago: "Suddenly she remembered. When she had sat there last ten years ago there had been a little sprig or leaf pattern on the table-cloth, which she had looked at in a moment of revelation. There had been a problem about a foreground of a picture. . . . She would paint that picture now." We have reached the time of the resumption and completion of old initiatives.

Beginning is not so easy for Lily, even though she feels she is closer to the solution now. The white canvas is as daunting as ever. More daunting still is Mr. Ramsay. For some reason nothing can be seriously ventured so long as he is still on the premises, almost as if his analytic spirit represents a force inimical to all creative focus. "Let him be fifty feet away," thinks Lily, "let him not even speak to you, let him not even see you, he permeated, he prevailed, he imposed himself. He changed everything."

But at last Mr. Ramsay and his son and daughter set off, and Lily bears down on her project, aligning memory with the abstract disposition of line, shape, and color. The very act of painting is for her a working together of past and present, of feeling and pigment. "Out and out one went, further and further, until at last one seemed to be on a narrow plank, perfectly alone, over the sea. And as she dipped into the blue paint, she dipped too into the past there." The dynamic builds, gathers momentum, her glimpses of the Ramsays' boat growing smaller in the distance somehow intensifying her access. Its location on the water becomes vitally linked to her sense of progress (so much so that an unexpected shift in position briefly destroys her sense of balance), the pitch of her engagement intensifying as she works, bringing her into a state of almost hallucinatory recall, very nearly restoring Mrs. Ramsay to her sight. This sense of intimation, coming in the throes of her creative absorption, fills Lily with such longing that she almost believes that if she calls out to her she will appear, a kind of ultimate redemption of vanished time. And she does. "'Mrs. Ramsay!' she said aloud, 'Mrs. Ramsay!' The tears ran down her face."

But no. Mrs. Ramsay must remain as she is, perished, and Lily must express the loss of her being—the desire for her presence—through the shapes on the canvas.

Then, perfectly synchronized, in a lyrical convergence such as never quite happens in real life, the two narrative lines come together. As the Ramsays reach the lighthouse, closing the circle begun all those years ago when James was just a little boy, Lily finds her completing gesture: "With a sudden intensity, as if she saw it clear for a second, she drew a line there, in the centre. It was done; it was finished. Yes, she thought, laying down her brush in extreme fatigue, I have had my vision." And the drawing of the line, the attaining of the vision, also marks the conclusion of the novel, brilliantly fusing the painting with the novel that describes it, fusing the imagined with the actual, pulling all the elements together as into a vortex and then collapsing that into a point. As Lily's creative intuition—and love—finally contain and express the life of the Ramsays, so Woolf has placed her character, one among many, in an imagined space that composed itself from everything she knew and remembered of her own family and past. I don't know that art can catch hold of the subjective sense of the past any more intensely.

Woolf's deepest desire was to achieve restoration by finding some balance, if not effective union, between opposing temperaments; by allowing impulses from the past to complete themselves in the present; and by trusting in the synthetic reality of Lily's artistic vision, if not the artistic work itself. For me, her reader, returning to *To the Lighthouse* years after my original encounter, there were other kinds of reconciliation. None of these are obvious or easy to summarize, but they involve a somewhat parallel process of bringing my understandings and memories forward in time, allowing loss to be re-lived, but also to be set against a more recent realization: what was once a true happiness was not, as first feared, entirely canceled by its loss. Rather—and here I think of the survival of the spirit of Mrs. Ramsay in the memories and actions of others—that experience survives in us transformed, putting light influential pressure on our daily lives. My long-ago relationship with Jess, the feelings of it so grown together with this book, resurfaced as part of my reading. And because I know how intently she once absorbed these pages, how sympathetic she was to Mrs. Ramsay—the great sympathetic presence—I get a sense of expanded dimension, of a connectedness at once chimerical and real, which has to be the aim of any artist looking to reincarnate the most vital elements of her experience.

To the Lighthouse allowed me to summon up an old relationship and somewhat integrate its loss. For that alone I value it above most other novels. But it reached me in another, more impersonal way as well. Through the extraordinary precision of her lyricism—a lyricism far more intense than what I myself aspire to—Woolf enlarged my sense of possibility. More even than James Joyce, whose *Ulysses* she deplored as vulgar, she showed how nuanced a work of prose could be, how accurately an interior shift or a sensuous particular could be registered. As much as Joyce, she made the intensities of the psychological life viable for literature. This does not mean that a writer has to strive for comparable effects in order to profit from her example. For me—I am *not* a fiction writer—the work and writer became talismanic. If I focus intently on the thought of either, I experience a release of energy, a renewed excitement about the possibilities of the written word. Moreover, I remember, if I have through frustration or inattention let it slip away, that language used with inspired intent is fully adequate to life as we both live and dream it.

The Tether of Origins

Alice Munro's *The Beggar Maid: Stories of Flo and Rose*

I FIND THAT the older I get the less interested I am in literary accounts of self-making and coming-of-age. Not that I'm ever immune to the dramas of the susceptible "I" in its early encounters with the turbulence of the world, but having for better or worse "made" myself, most of it, I am more intent now on the lower-definition business of coping, carrying on, and sustaining an original passion through the long haul. I tune in not to see, again, how people fall in love (though who can look away?), but to understand how they fortify themselves in its aftermath; not how they find and get, but how they hold onto it, and how they deal with letting go.

I became aware of this decisive shift of focus when I returned to Alice Munro's *The Beggar Maid: Stories of Flo and Rose,* which I first read in my thirties. I was then working as a clerk in a bookstore and a customer made some remark about it that sent me right over to the M's of the Fiction section. I was completely taken, not just by a voice that registered life in the same way I did, but also by the fact that the author was a woman. I was not used to finding what I thought of as my particular alienated romanticism mirrored back to me by a female sensibility. I loved Munro's prose, her way with place and atmosphere; I especially loved that she understood how the past continually impinges on, and sometimes completely overpowers, the awareness of the present.

That said, I was still more engaged by the earlier Rose stories—the ones that featured her growing up and setting forth. The later, more outwardly settled stories seemed to me lacking in narrative tension. What a surprise now, two decades later, to feel how decisively the center of gravity has moved, to discover what emotional saturations these ostensibly quieter stories carry.

The Beggar Maid, one of Munro's earliest books, is that strange quantity, a collection of individual stories that has the afterlife of a novel. In part this has to do with specific structural overlaps and the development of a psychologically cumulative story line. But even more the feeling grows out of what the reader feels as a sustained pressure of intent. Munro was, I'm convinced, using displacement and strategic transposition to write the ghost-narrative of her own life to date. Putting to the page, that is, not her own life, but the near-miss, the there-but-for-the-grace-of . . . whatever it is that finally determines our special track through the world.

I'm not suggesting any specific commonalities between Munro's life and the experience she gives her protagonist Rose, though she has borrowed from her own store of the real—every fiction writer does this. My assertion, based mainly on the pricking of my intuition, is that she wrote what amounts to a parallel narrative in order to discover the life that only the gift—and discipline—of art saved her from.

Munro came to writing fairly late, and for a long time before she fully claimed that alternate channel for herself, she felt herself immured in the pre-liberation conventions of her generation. What an extraordinary thing it must have been, then, to find and follow the path of art, and then—imagine—to feel the accelerating growth of the gift, past all expectation. This has to be as frightening as it is exhilarating—frightening precisely because it carries intimations of an intended life, a destiny. But intended how, why, and determined by what ulterior agency? My guess is that in the grip of this most private recognition the other "almost" life has to become more vivid: the writer is compelled to brood over it as anyone would brood over a calamity just barely avoided.

I sometimes think that this is the secret impetus behind John Updike's Rabbit books—writing as a way of congratulating oneself on the great good luck of the vocation found, and of revisiting the alternative in order to keep that pleasure alive. But also—and this is true of both Updike and Munro, I think—writing has to be a way of touching wood, of conferring ongoing benediction on that other self, out of natural compassion, but also to avoid the hubris that could call down the wrath of the gods. The same gods who bestowed the artistic gift—which is too considerable and clear to have come from the chaos of the self. For this reason, Munro's stories about Rose, though they are not about writing in any obvious way, represent an ongoing meditation on the grace of the gift.

I put forward this interpretation because it helps explain to me my own strong connection to this book, a connection far stronger than what the individual narratives would warrant. Reading *The Beggar Maid*, responding to it as a novel, a unified entity, I feel meditatively engaged in the theme of possibility, better able to carry on the irresistible personal speculations on the "what if?" which is what the reading of almost any fiction invites. I don't mean just the crazy-making game of factoring instances: what if I had made this choice, or that; what if I had had gone here, not there? I also mean locating myself in the metaphysical category of the possible, the worldview in which all variables are always in play and that we choose ourselves moment by moment and abide the consequences of our choices. I feel this strongly when I read these linked accounts of Munro's Rose, and at the same time I feel the reverse, especially the second time through: how, choose as we will, we cannot step free of our fate—what emerges only in retrospect as the inevitable life our character and our origins have prescribed for us.

THE BEGGAR MAID groups ten stories around a single protagonist, Rose, who grows up in the small Ontario town of Hanratty, goes away to college, marries her college beau, Patrick, and then lives for a time in Vancouver, where she raises a daughter and begins a career as an actress and television interviewer. Later, after she and Patrick divorce, Rose moves from place to place, having occasional love affairs but remaining essentially unattached, which is where Munro leaves her at the end of the last chronological story. Some of this echoes the author's own vita, much of it does not.

IF PLOT, or narrative through-line, were the main criterion for novelistic integrity, then *The Beggar Maid* would not qualify. The stories reveal much about the fate of one character over time, but they are centripetal, freestanding; plotting their larger arc point to point does not reveal any progressive tension. The collection is not, in any traditional outward sense, novelistic.

Yet I do think that *The Beggar Maid* can be read in this larger, more encompassing—and gratifying—way, so long as we expand somewhat our genre definition to include other notions of unity. Consistency of sensibility is one such, and the collection is without question cut from a single cloth, in that it not only sustains an essentially unified tone, but also keeps a relatively fixed authorial distance from its several recurrent characters, Rose foremost among them. In my view, Munro manages to have it both ways: the stories can stand by themselves, each furnishing its own necessary narrative context, but they also carry elements from one to the next that complicate and intensify Munro's presentation of Rose's life if we choose to read in sequence.

Munro's treatment of the character of Flo, Rose's stepmother, offers a good instance of this effect. While the book's subtitle—*Stories of Flo and Rose*—would suggest that Flo gets marquee billing, this is not really the case. She is a central presence in the earliest stories, in the first "Royal Beatings," in particular, but her influence recedes conspicuously after Rose moves away from Hanratty. In most of the later stories she is an episodically invoked memory at most. Still, she somehow earns her titular importance and her appearances and disappearances give us insight into Munro's overall structural method and add to the argument for viewing the collection as a tightly bounded whole, if not a standard novel.

I stay on this because the distinction is important to me. My investment in *The Beggar Maid* has much to do with Munro's representation of changing inner experience over the course of a life, and particularly the workings of memory, and I can't help but assume a larger intended unity. I see, over and above creating the self-contained world of each separate story, a consistent expression of a single subjectivity moving through time. For whatever reason, I connect to this life, its standoffish vigilance, among other things. These are my moods, my sulks, my good resolutions, my vanities and fantasies of self-redemption, my regrets—or at least they're close enough to compel my best attention.

Munro's trick is to narrate in the third person, but in such a way that we develop the kind of intimate grounding that is more often the achievement of first-person narration. She does this by handling in an ongoing credible way the kinds of recognitions that we come to associate with the sensibility of Rose, thus gradually embedding us in her unique point of view. Although she is a narrated character, we come to feel her life with unusual immediacy. Munro's treatment of Flo in relation to Rose illustrates the method perfectly.

The first story, "Royal Beatings," is the densest, the most "written" of the ten, using a lyric compression and an associative structure to create its own contained reality. Linked sections of anecdote and exposition give us a collage portrait of Rose's world, including a fairly immediate sense of Hanratty—West Hanratty, the less well-to-do part of town, especially— some familiarity with the town's characters and legends, and a sharply etched introduction to the family: Rose's father, her stepmother Flo, and her stepbrother Brian, all of whom, I should note, figure without repeated background introductions in the rest of the stories.

The other anomalous feature of "Royal Beatings" is that on this one occasion Flo is given equal standing with Rose. Flo steps forward as a fully drawn domestic antagonist, a counterfigure whose interactions and conflicts with Rose bring her to life on the page at the same time as they help underscore her stepdaughter's dreamy and subtly willful character. The rest of *The Beggar Maid* could be said to develop and explore what is first set down in this intense chamber-work narration. The resolution of this story, moreover, is our first introduction to Munro's signature "denouement" strategy, which the reader gradually incorporates as a feature of Rose's, rather than the author's, vision of life.

Royal Beating. That was Flo's promise. You are going to get one Royal Beating.

The word Royal lolled on Flo's tongue, took on trappings. Rose had a need to picture things, to pursue absurdities, that was stronger than the need to stay out of trouble, and instead of taking this threat to heart she pondered: how is a beating royal? She came up with a tree-lined avenue, a crowd of formal spectators, some

white horses and black slaves. Someone knelt, and the blood came leaping out like banners. An occasion both savage and splendid.
In real life they didn't approach such dignity, and it was only Flo who tried to supply the event with some high air of necessity and regret. Rose and her father soon got beyond anything presentable.

That there will be conflict between Flo and someone in her power is clear by the end of the third short sentence—that that someone is Rose is obvious soon after. The rest of this opening passage gives the first impression of the girl, one that becomes like a platform for all of our later determinations. Rose is her own person, dreamy, imaginative, and not much cowed by Flo's threats. At the same time there are hints of a certain dramatic collusion, an acquiescence by Rose to Flo's need to act out her tensions and anxieties, which is, we come to see, also an intensification of Rose's sense of private superiority.

"Royal Beatings" uses a basic counterpoint strategy to create her tensions, at the same time setting the tone for the stories that follow, introducing the four family characters and evoking memorably idiosyncratic impressions of the small-town world that will be a steady backdrop reference throughout the life Rose makes for herself.

The central narrative—the point to which the counterpoint responds—involves the skirmishes between daughter and stepmother. "What do they have to say to each other? It doesn't really matter. Flo speaks of Rose's smart-aleck behavior, rudeness and sloppiness and conceit. Her willingness to make work for others, her lack of gratitude. She mentions Brian's innocence, Rose's corruption." Flo's gathering recriminations eventually excite her to such a pitch that she calls her husband, Rose's father, to punish the girl with a "beating." The build-up, and then the carefully choreographed event (everyone knows that the blows are held back, struck more for show than anything else) and its aftermath, tell much about relations in the family; we see, for one thing, how the histrionic and extroverted Flo rules over father and daughter, who are linked in our minds through their distractedness and their love for odd words and arresting expressions ("Macaroni, pepperoni, Botticelli, beans—" Rose overhears her father muttering as he works). What's more, the beating episode exposes the family's habits and rituals, their special way of shuttling between on-stage and off-stage behaviors. The to-and-fro, a practical necessity since the front part of their house is a small general store tended mainly by Flo, also maps a strong psychological division in Rose between what is concealed and what is shown.

The counterpoint narrative, really a kind of local-historical aside, is triggered by the presence in the store of Becky Tyde, one of the town's familiar unfortunates:

> She was big-headed loud-voiced dwarf, with a mascot's sexless swagger, a red velvet tam, a twisted neck that forced her to hold her head on one side, always looking up and sideways. . . . Rose watched her shoes, being scared of the rest of her, of her laugh and her neck. She knew from Flo that Becky Tyde had been sick with polio as a child. . . . It was hard to believe that she had started out differently, that she had ever been normal.

Munro relates, as part of the known Hanratty lore, the story of how Becky Tyde's father had brutalized all of his children, until certain "influential and respectable" men arranged to have old man Tyde horsewhipped. But the three enlisted local thugs, including one "Hat" Nettleton, let things get out of hand, and Becky's father died soon after from his injuries.

Munro invokes the frontier-day mythology of old rough unsocialized Hanratty, a mythology that then lingers just behind the agitated scene between Flo and Rose and Rose's father. We're meant to take in the almost ironic congruence and to underline the difference: the Saturday drama at Rose's house is finally marked by all kinds of capitulations and reparations that not only soften the blow, but reveal it to be a genuine, if dysfunctional, ritual of connection. It is, we sense, a familiar pattern. When the crisis passes, for instance, Flo brings a meal on a tray to Rose in her room. Writes Munro:

> Flo will come up and get the tray. She may say, "I see you got your appetite still," or "Did you like the chocolate milk, was it enough syrup in it?" depending on how chastened she is feeling, herself. At any rate, all advantage will be lost. Rose will understand that life has started up again, that they will all sit around the table

eating again, listening to the radio news. . . . They will be embarrassed, but rather less than you might expect considering how they have behaved. They will feel a queer lassitude, a convalescent indolence, not far off satisfaction.

My home situation was outwardly nothing like what Munro has created here, but I'm electrified as I read. Not just because the scene is so skillfully choreographed, but also because these are, reconfigured, psychological and emotional dynamics I recognize very well. The division of roles between parents, for instance: my father's sharp punitive authority counterbalanced by my mother's subtle intercessions, her shuttle diplomacy, how after putting balm on the worst of what had been inflicted, she set about contriving the restoration of the *status quo ante*.

At this point, for all its shrewd characterization and discharge of tension, the story is unfinished; it still awaits Munro's distinctive intervention, the move that reminds us that there is an author behind the scenes, holding this whole world in the suspension of her imagination. What follows will become a kind of copyrighted narrative move for Munro, an unexpected—and revealing—leap forward in time.

"Years later," she writes, "many years later, on a Sunday morning, Rose turned on the radio." Rose is by this point a mature woman, decades out of Hanratty, living by herself in Toronto. She finds herself listening to a broadcast interview that almost sounds to her like a scene from a play. "The old man's voice was so vain and belligerent, the interviewer's quite helpless and alarmed, under its practiced gentleness and ease."

> "You had a lot of experiences young men growing up today
> will never have." [the interviewer coaches]. . . "Can you recall any
> of them for us?"
>
> *I eaten groundhog meat one time. One winter. You wouldna cared
> for it. Heh.*
>
> There was a pause, of appreciation, it would seem, then the
> announcer's voice saying that the foregoing had been an interview
> with Mr. Wilfred Nettleton of Hanratty, Ontario, made on his

hundred and second birthday, two weeks before his death, last
spring. A living link with our past. Mr. Nettleton had been inter-
viewed in the Wawanash County Home for the Aged.
Hat Nettleton.
Horsewhipper into centenarian.

Yes, we remember now—Hat had been one of the group that beat
Becky Tyde's father to the point of death. Rose registers the great surprise—
material from her first life is suddenly injected into her present. Rose longs
to tell someone—she longs to tell Flo. Flo, the abrasive, aggressive, cajol-
ing, and gossipy woman who had raised her is the one person, it turns out,
who could relish the scandalous irony of it all.

But Flo was in the same place Hat Nettleton had died in, and
there wasn't any way Rose could reach her. She had been there even
when that interview was recorded, though she would not have
heard it, would not have known about it. After Rose put her in the
Home, a couple of years earlier, she had stopped talking. She had
removed herself, and spent most of her time sitting in a corner of
her crib, looking crafty and disagreeable, not answering anybody,
though she occasionally showed her feelings by biting a nurse.

Munro's unexpected thrust into the future is a surefire way to bring
complexity and fresh resonance into the story. Not only does it deliver
the tragicomic irony of hindsight—that Hat should be seen as a venerable
elder, that Flo should have completely lost her vigilant edge to the insults
of age—but it somehow bestows the power of that recognition on Rose.
Munro writes the story, but its deepest writerly understandings become
those of her proxy, her stand-in, the girl who shares aspects of her own
early life. As for the ancient basic standoff between Flo and Rose—it is
finally just the passing of time that resolves things. Like Chekhov, Munro
grants as much power to unforeseeable circumstance as she does to the
actions of her characters, a strategy that almost invariably yields up irony,
for outcomes are so seldom as willed or expected.

These forward projections of Munro's have the same emotional potency as well-managed flashbacks. They cross-section a life and put us face to face with time, the wrenching sense of its never-again as well as the recognition of constant surprise that makes that sense just bearable. I have that penchant. As kids whirl around and around so they can watch the ceiling spin, so I sometimes feed myself on images of passing time—photographs, documents, artifacts, whatever will fan up the "that was then, this is now" awareness. I subject myself masochistically to the certainty of change and loss, which is finally maybe less like twirling and more like holding the hand closer and closer to a lit match, to see how much I can stand, to feel more alive on the leading edge of the pain. Munro delivers a sense of this through the construction of her stories, staging the subtle instances of Rose's vertigo, her repeated recognition of the mysterious saturations of time.

Several other stories from Rose's school years, "Privilege" and "Half a Grapefruit," also feature the Flo and Rose dynamic, both concluding with an abrupt leap forward in time to show what became of the principal characters.

"Wild Swans," by contrast, recounts with a tense moment-by-moment escalation, an anonymous sexual encounter on a train. Rose, on her way to Toronto for the first time alone, finds herself seated beside a man who may or may not be a priest. Once the journey gets underway, he begins an artful assault, casual "accidental" touch leading, with Rose's implicit, but tormented consent, to a more invasive groping. "She was concentrating on that leg, that bit of skin with stocking over it. She could not bring herself to look. Was there a pressure, or was there not?" The contact is completely anonymous, never acknowledged, and quite erotic in its way of managing repression and release. The episode marks at one and the same time Rose's sexual initiation and her departure from insular Hanratty, functioning in the book as a kind of pivot, or hinged-door opening onto the larger world.

The title story, "The Beggar Maid," follows in discontinuous segments the trajectory of a relationship, from first meeting and courtship to marriage, motherhood, and eventual acrimonious divorce. Munro tracks Rose over the course of several years, as she moves from fresh college innocence to fully experienced (and eventually disillusioned) maturity. It's the first—

the decisive—relationship. But the presentation is less an exploration of the actual interactions of Rose and Patrick, and more about failures, the ways in which others can never reach her, relationships never satisfy. When at story's end—another forward flash—Rose sees Patrick at an airport, they are long since separated. We feel that she has traversed the full coming-of-age path. "He made a face at her. It was a truly hateful, savagely warning, face; infantile, self-indulgent, yet calculated; it was a timed explosion of disgust and loathing." We can only guess at the betrayals and disappointments that created that expression.

The remaining five stories have the feel of denouement about them. On first reading, these reports on adulthood seemed flatter, lacking the jumped-up energy and uncertainty that depictions of character-in-formation deliver. Taken together they gave the clear message that adulthood itself *is* denouement, showing us an entirely different field of possibility. But these were to be for me the late-arriving satisfactions of the book, packed with nuances I'd missed when I read through as a younger man. I didn't miss them because I read past them, though, but because I hadn't accumulated certain kinds of knowledge yet. I didn't have the perspective to see how people keep resurfacing in our lives, or how seemingly small accommodations grow in implication, or how the outlook of things in the present is altered by a more realistic understanding of what the future holds, that time in which everything was once felt to be possible. Where before I saw the book as trailing off in the second half, losing the sharp edge—and interest—of Rose's awakening self, now I can see clearly how the girl and the young woman prefigure the disillusioned Rose of later days.

The later stories may deal with adult situations (I mean this in the nonsensational way), but they keep pointing us back to origins, reminding us over and over that the past is a gravitational field almost impossible to escape—a bit of wisdom unavailable to anyone who is not old enough to have tried and tried. Even more, they bring the hard news that the early formations of character are almost always carried through, that they determine much about the destinies that may sometimes appear to befall individuals arbitrarily.

Rose is very much the same person throughout the stories, certainly in this more psychologically grounded way I'm talking about. The dreamy, unsatisfied girl of "Royal Beatings" is now a somewhat less distracted, somewhat more dissatisfied woman. She is sharply split, then as now, between her performing social identity and her nervous, vulnerable private self. Before, in the home and school worlds, she shuttled between her asserted attitudes (the "airs" she often put on) and her sharp self-lacerations when she was alone. Success—the achievement of a certain renown—has not really altered this. The gulf between public and private selves is probably as great as ever. The difference, no small thing finally, is that as she gets older Rose is less and less willing to exert the energy to hold up appearances—the weight of the façade seems too much.

"Who Do You Think You Are?" is the final story in the collection, and it brings the cycle to a powerful and poignant close, returning the prodigal to her Hanratty roots and underscoring, as the title itself signals, that, contra Thomas Wolfe's declaration, you not only can, you *must* go home again.

In a move that closely recalls the Becky Tyde subplot of "Royal Beatings," the story opens with Rose and her stepbrother Brian as adults reminiscing about another of the town's unfortunates, Milton Homer. Nobody knew exactly what was wrong with Milton, but when Brian's wife Phoebe refers to him as the "village idiot," both Rose and Brian affirm that they had never heard him called that. "If it was necessary to describe Milton to an outsider," Munro writes, "people would say that he was 'not all there.'" His behavior was ungoverned. Back when Hanratty held parades, Milton would invariably appear in the midst of things and act outrageously. "Behind the Black Knights he would pull a dour face, and hold his head as if a top hat was riding on it; behind the ladies he wiggled his hips and diddled an imaginary sunshade." Like Becky Tyde, he was, for Rose, an extrusion of the old unreconstructed Hanratty, a blot on the idea of civic order. But he was also somehow part of the town's identity, a vivid but nonthreatening presence collectively claimed as "one of ours." He is now a direct feeling-link to the past.

Rose's recollection of Milton starts a chain of association that then takes in his two guardian aunts, Miss Hattie, Rose's teacher, and her "stay-at-home twin," Miss Mattie. It is the former who one day in class upbraids the girl for getting above herself by quickly memorizing an assigned poem. "'You can't go thinking you are better than other people just because you can learn poems,'" she says. "'Who do you think you are?'"

For us, the question goes straight to the heart of Rose's character. In story after story, situation after situation, we have seen her behave with concealed entitlement, secret grandiosity, looking down on Flo, separating herself out from the girls in her school, daring to imagine a romantic future for herself away from Hanratty, pursuing affairs, always with the conviction that hers is to be a better lot. At the end of this last story Munro will make it clear—again—that she is wrong.

Through memories of Homer and Miss Hattie we come to Ralph Gillespie, Rose's classmate, the one boy with whom she feels a quiet—and unspoken—bond. Ralph makes himself known to others as a mimic, surprising the whole class one day by getting Milton Homer: ". . . he was very good; his large, pale, good-natured face took on the lumpy desperation of Milton's; his eyes goggled and his jowls shook and his words came out in a hoarse hypnotized singsong." And: "Rose never quite got over a comradely sort of apprehension on his behalf. She had another feeling as well, not envy, but a shaky sort of longing. She wanted to do the same. Not Milton Homer; she did not want to do Milton Homer. She wanted to fill up in that magical, releasing way, transform herself; she wanted the courage and the power." I can't help but read this as Munro's shorthand description of the dream of the would-be artist, the writer—my self-created "true" Rose.

Ralph, unbeknownst to himself, in the way that happens over and over in the life of the thinking/dreaming person, has found his way into Rose's privacy, her dreaming solitude. It doesn't finally matter that they scarcely acknowledge each other all these years. Because of Ralph, who he is, what he can do, she feels known, her isolation somehow divided and shared. And then, just like that, Ralph leaves school and Rose loses contact. She moves away. And one would say, were it not Munro, "end of story." But through the agency of a late-story flash-forward Ralph comes back into her life.

The story moves to conclusion as Rose returns to Hanratty to put Flo

in the County Home (where, we recall, she left her at the end of "Royal
Beatings") and to ready the house for sale. While she is in town she is
taken to the Legion Hall by Flo's neighbors, and there, so many years after
Miss Hattie's classroom, after so much turbulent life, she meets Ralph
again—"a thin, gray-haired man holding a mug of beer." Writes Munro:
"If Rose had met him on the street she would not have recognized him,
he would have been a stranger to her, but after she had looked at him for
a moment he seemed quite unchanged to her, unchanged from himself at
seventeen or fifteen, his gray hair which had been light brown still falling
over his forehead, his face still pale and calm and rather large for his body,
the same diffident, watchful, withholding look." She is priming us, setting
us up, getting us to half-believe, as Rose does, that on a deeper level nothing ever really changes, that passing years are a chimera, and that what
ultimately matters are the few fresh essences we are allowed to apprehend:
"Rose and Ralph Gillespie looked at each other. There was the same silent
joke, the same conspiracy, comfort; the same, the same." They trade news,
banter, and Rose keeps registering some undercurrent. "All the time she
talked," writes Munro, "she was wondering what he wanted her to say. He
did want something. But he would not make any move to get it. Her first
impression of him, as boyishly shy and ingratiating, had to change. That
was his surface. Underneath he was self-sufficient, resigned to living in
bafflement, perhaps proud. She wished that he would speak to her from
that level, and she thought he wished it, too, but they were prevented."

Ralph is almost a confessor-figure to her, a man implicitly so attuned
to her proud and vain and uncertain self that in his presence she feels
paradoxically released to herself. How does this work? Remembering their
conversation later, Rose reflects:

> Everything she had done could sometimes be seen as a mistake.
> She had never felt this more strongly than when she was talking
> to Ralph Gillespie, but when she thought about him afterward
> her mistakes appeared unimportant. She was enough a child of
> her time to wonder if what she felt about him was simply sexual
> warmth, sexual curiosity; she did not think it was. There seemed

to be feelings which could only be spoken of in translation; perhaps they could only be acted on in translation; not speaking of
them and not acting on them is the right course to take because
translation is dubious. Dangerous, as well.

Of course, nothing comes of the encounter—nothing could. Ralph
remains Rose's secret sharer, and when she learns of his death, deemed
accidental, from the Hanratty paper, she makes no mention of it to Brian
or Phoebe.

> Rose didn't tell this to anybody, glad that there was one thing at
> least she wouldn't spoil by telling, though she knew it was a lack
> of material as much as honorable restraint that kept her quiet.
> What could she say about herself and Ralph Gillespie, except that
> she felt his life, close, closer than the lives of men she'd loved, one
> slot over from her own?

What a perfect balance, to have the interrogation of the title, "Who
Do You Think You Are?" the shameful mantra of Rose's troubled, if also
successful, life, answered so obliquely. In what becomes a circular sort of
resolution, Rose is returned to her beginnings and allowed some of the
peace of private self-acceptance. In a person she barely knows, but whom
she knows in some other way better than she knows anyone, she finds her
isolation obliquely—very obliquely—redeemed. When I read this ending,
and I do return to it from time to time, I feel a private rush of connection. The episode, the recognition, catches hold of so much that is familiar from my inchoate inner life, the part of the self that mulls and muses,
wondering "what if?" and imagining different outcomes along the roads
not taken. This is not the thinking self, but a part of the "I" even more
basic and familiar, one that comes fully awake only in the dream of a
book. If there is a bridging that art accomplishes, this is it. What Munro
has brought to life in the imagined life of Rose has in some uncanny way
touched off my most private recognitions; her compensatory other life
has clarified my progress in this one right here.

SVEN BIRKERTS is the author of six books, including *The Gutenberg Elegies: The Fate of Reading in an Electronic Age, Readings,* and *My Sky Blue Trades: Growing Up Counter in a Contrary Time.* He has been the editor of *AGNI* since July 2002 and has received grants from the Lila Wallace-Reader's Digest Foundation and the Guggenheim Foundation. He won the Citation for Excellence in Reviewing from the National Book Critics Circle in 1985 and the Spielvogel-Diamonstein Award from PEN for the best book of essays in 1990. Birkerts has reviewed regularly for the *New York Times Book Review,* the *New Republic, Esquire,* the *Washington Post,* the *Atlantic, Mirabella, Parnassus,* the *Yale Review,* and other publications. He is a member of the core faculty of the Bennington Writing Seminars and has taught at Emerson College, Amherst College, and Mt. Holyoke College. Birkerts is currently the Briggs-Copeland lecturer at Harvard University and lives in Arlington, Massachusetts, with his wife and two children.

The text of *Reading Life* has been set in Adobe Garamond Pro, drawn by Robert Slimbach and based on type cut by Claude Garamond in the sixteenth century. Book design by Wendy Holdman. Composition by Prism Publishing Center, Minneapolis, Minnesota. Manufactured by Versa Press, Inc. on acid-free paper.